MW01026739

READINGS ON

WUTHERING HEIGHTS

OTHER TITLES IN THE GREENHAVEN PRESS LITERARY COMPANION SERIES:

AMERICAN AUTHORS

Maya Angelou
Stephen Crane
Emily Dickinson
William Faulkner
F. Scott Fitzgerald
Nathaniel Hawthorne
Ernest Hemingway
Herman Melville
Arthur Miller
Eugene O'Neill
Edgar Allan Poe
John Steinbeck
Mark Twain
Thornton Wilder

AMERICAN LITERATURE

The Adventures of
  Huckleberry Finn
The Adventures of Tom
  Sawyer
The Catcher in the Rye
The Crucible
Death of a Salesman
The Glass Menagerie
The Grapes of Wrath
The Great Gatsby
Of Mice and Men
The Old Man and the Sea
The Pearl
The Scarlet Letter
A Separate Peace

BRITISH AUTHORS

Jane Austen
Joseph Conrad
Charles Dickens

BRITISH LITERATURE

Animal Farm
Beowulf
The Canterbury Tales
Great Expectations
Hamlet
Julius Caesar
Lord of the Flies
Macbeth
Pride and Prejudice
Romeo and Juliet
Shakespeare: The Comedies
Shakespeare: The Histories
Shakespeare: The Sonnets
Shakespeare: The Tragedies
A Tale of Two Cities

WORLD AUTHORS

Fyodor Dostoyevsky
Homer
Sophocles

WORLD LITERATURE

All Quiet on the Western
  Front
The Diary of a Young Girl
A Doll's House

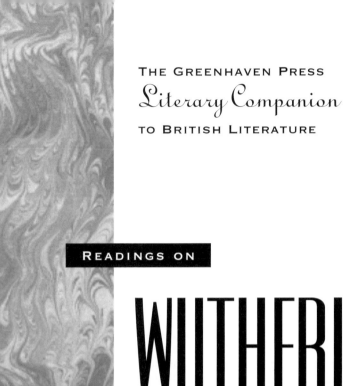

THE GREENHAVEN PRESS
Literary Companion
TO BRITISH LITERATURE

READINGS ON

WUTHERING HEIGHTS

Hayley R. Mitchell, *Book Editor*

David L. Bender, *Publisher*
Bruno Leone, *Executive Editor*
Bonnie Szumski, *Series Editor*

Greenhaven Press, Inc., San Diego, CA

Library of Congress Cataloging-in-Publication Data

Readings on Wuthering Heights / Hayley R. Mitchell,
    book editor.
        p.   cm. — (The Greenhaven Press literary
    companion to British literature)
        Includes bibliographical references and index.
        ISBN 1-56510-833-7 (lib. bdg. : alk. paper). —
    ISBN 1-56510-832-9 (pbk. : alk. paper)
        1. Brontë, Emily, 1818–1848. Wuthering Heights.
    I. Mitchell, Hayley R., 1968–   . II. Series.
    PR4172.W73R43   1999
    823'.8—dc21   98-28876
                                                        CIP

Cover photo: Photofest

I lingered around them, under that benign sky; watched the moths fluttering among the heath and harebells, listened to the soft wind breathing through the grass, and wondered how any one could ever imagine unquiet slumbers for the sleepers in that quiet earth.

—Emily Brontë
from Wuthering Heights

CONTENTS

characters, he is the only one who redeems himself by eventually renouncing his violent ways.

FOREWORD

"'Tis the good reader that
makes the good book."

Ralph Waldo Emerson

The story's bare facts are simple: The captain, an old and scarred seafarer, walks with a peg leg made of whale ivory. He relentlessly drives his crew to hunt the world's oceans for the great white whale that crippled him. After a long search, the ship encounters the whale and a fierce battle ensues. Finally the captain drives his harpoon into the whale, but the harpoon line catches the captain about the neck and drags him to his death.

A simple story, a straightforward plot—yet, since the 1851 publication of Herman Melville's *Moby-Dick*, readers and critics have found many meanings in the struggle between Captain Ahab and the whale. To some, the novel is a cautionary tale that depicts how Ahab's obsession with revenge leads to his insanity and death. Others believe that the whale represents the unknowable secrets of the universe and that Ahab is a tragic hero who dares to challenge fate by attempting to discover this knowledge. Perhaps Melville intended Ahab as a criticism of Americans' tendency to become involved in well-intentioned but irrational causes. Or did Melville model Ahab after himself, letting his fictional character express his anger at what he perceived as a cruel and distant god?

Although literary critics disagree over the meaning of *Moby-Dick*, readers do not need to choose one particular interpretation in order to gain an understanding of Melville's novel. Instead, by examining various analyses, they can gain numerous insights into the issues that lie under the surface of the basic plot. Studying the writings of literary critics can also aid readers in making their own assessments of *Moby-Dick* and other literary works and in developing analytical thinking skills.

The Greenhaven Literary Companion Series was created with these goals in mind. Designed for young adults, this unique anthology series provides an engaging and comprehensive introduction to literary analysis and criticism. The essays included in the Literary Companion Series are chosen for their accessibility to a young adult audience and are expertly edited in consideration of both the reading and comprehension levels of this audience. In addition, each essay is introduced by a concise summation that presents the contributing writer's main themes and insights. Every anthology in the Literary Companion Series contains a varied selection of critical essays that cover a wide time span and express diverse views. Wherever possible, primary sources are represented through excerpts from authors' notebooks, letters, and journals and through contemporary criticism.

Each title in the Literary Companion Series pays careful consideration to the historical context of the particular author or literary work. In-depth biographies and detailed chronologies reveal important aspects of authors' lives and emphasize the historical events and social milieu that influenced their writings. To facilitate further research, every anthology includes primary and secondary source bibliographies of articles and/or books selected for their suitability for young adults. These engaging features make the Greenhaven Literary Companion series ideal for introducing students to literary analysis in the classroom or as a library resource for young adults researching the world's great authors and literature.

Exceptional in its focus on young adults, the Greenhaven Literary Companion Series strives to present literary criticism in a compelling and accessible format. Every title in the series is intended to spark readers' interest in leading American and world authors, to help them broaden their understanding of literature, and to encourage them to formulate their own analyses of the literary works that they read. It is the editors' hope that young adult readers will find these anthologies to be true companions in their study of literature.

INTRODUCTION

Wuthering Heights is difficult to limit to a particular genre of fiction, as it does not grow out of a single literary tradition. It contains elements of Romantic fiction in its emphasis on folklore and the supernatural; Gothic fiction in its demonic portrayal of Heathcliff and the themes of imprisonment; and Victorian Domestic fiction, in which idyllic family and community relationships are the ultimate goal. In its combination of these traditions, and others, *Wuthering Heights* is in no way a conventional novel for its time.

Not only are readers unable to tether the novel's conventions to a single literary genre, but many also often feel disconnected from, or baffled by, the events of the book, much as its early reviewers felt. As readers of *Wuthering Heights* we neither recognize ourselves in Brontë's impassioned, sometimes frightening characters, nor identify with their surroundings, the howling moors. It is doubtful, too, that readers and the key inhabitants of these moors have experienced the same violence of emotions—the same burning desires—or acted on them with the same need to gain an absolute sense of control. As Virginia Woolf notes:

> There is no "I" in *Wuthering Heights*. There are no governesses. There are no employers. There is love, but it is not the love of men and women. Emily was inspired by some more general conception. The impulse, which urged her to create, was not her own suffering or her own injuries. She looked out upon a world cleft into gigantic disorder and felt within her the power to unite it in a book.[1]

What grows out of this power is a novel that is rich in language and complex in thought that covers the full spectrum of human emotions. While it is true we may not see *ourselves*, we do recognize the emotions—anger, revenge, lust, affection, grief, and love.

Each essay in this volume has aids for clear understanding. The introductions serve as directed reading for the essays by explaining main points, which are further identified by subheads within the essays. Footnotes identify uncommon references and define unfamiliar words. An occasional insert has been included to illustrate a point made in the essay or a feature of Brontë's prose. Taken together, these aids make the Greenhaven Press Literary Companion Series an indispensable research tool.

Readers return to *Wuthering Heights* because it is multifaceted; students not only of literature, but also of language, psychology, and life can study it on numerous levels. The novel, published over 150 years ago, has endured vast social, technological, scientific, and artistic changes that Emily Brontë perhaps could not have imagined. The novel survives because its power is not in the physical world of the novel, but in the forces behind the emotional one. "It is this suggestion of power underlying the apparitions of human nature, and lifting them up in the presence of greatness," Woolf writes, "that gives the book its huge stature among other novels."[2]

NOTES

1. Virginia Woolf, "*Jane Eyre* and *Wuthering Heights*," *The Common Reader: First Series.* New York: Harcourt Brace, 1925, p. 164.
2. Woolf, "*Jane Eyre* and *Wuthering Heights*," p. 164.

EMILY BRONTË: A BIOGRAPHY

Born on July 30, 1818, in England near the Yorkshire moors she would later romanticize in her only novel, *Wuthering Heights*, Emily Brontë was the fifth of six children born to Maria and Patrick Brontë, an Irish Anglican minister. Her other siblings were Maria, born in 1814, Elizabeth, born in 1815, Charlotte, born in 1816, Patrick, in 1817, and Anne, born in 1820. She was a reserved and silent girl who made few friends and was inclined toward homesickness, choosing to reject education outside the home to live among family and her beloved moors. Throughout her short life of thirty years, Brontë repeated the pattern of leaving home for schooling or employment opportunities only to return to Haworth (her father's parsonage since 1820) shortly after her departures. At Haworth she found comfort in her siblings and her surroundings, and it is here that she developed the imaginative, creative self that survives in her fiction and poetry today.

THE EARLY YEARS

In 1821, when Emily Brontë was three years old, her mother died of cancer. Elizabeth Branwell, the children's aunt, joined the household at that time, but it was Maria Brontë, the eldest sibling at eight years old, who seemingly took over the role of mother to the other children. At age six, Emily joined her three sisters at the Clergy Daughters' School at Cowan Bridge. It was her first educational experience outside the home. Tragically, illness struck the family again in 1825 when Maria and Elizabeth both died of tuberculosis contracted at school.

Upon the death of their sisters, Emily and her elder sister Charlotte were withdrawn from the Clergy Daughters' School. Emily was educated at home until her teen years but Charlotte left Haworth in 1831 to attend Roe Head School. At that time, Emily was "on the verge of adolescence," author Edward Chitham writes. Although Emily strengthened her bond with her younger sister Anne during this time, there is little evidence that she forged friendships outside the family. Instead, Chitham says, she became "introverted, self-divided and ill-at-ease with most other people."[1] After seven months at Roe Head, Charlotte returned home to further educate her sisters. Later, in 1835 when Emily was seventeen, Charlotte returned to Roe Head School as a governess.

Charlotte's move afforded Emily another opportunity for schooling outside the home. As part of Charlotte's governess contract, Emily was allowed to accompany her as a pupil. Emily only remained at Roe Head for three months, however, due to extreme homesickness. Author Richard Benvenuto writes that Emily could "survive and even flourish without her beloved Anne, but not without the freedom to range the moors and, more critically, not without Gondal," the fantasy-land she had created in stories written at Haworth. "The discipline at Roe Head was not harsh or demanding," Benvenuto continues, "but it drove a wedge between her and her imaginative life."[2]

Emily's emotional distress at Roe Head manifested itself in physical decline. Her body wasted away, and she feared she too suffered from the tuberculosis that had claimed the lives of her sisters. Modern scholars have speculated, however, that the condition may have been anorexia, a disorder that would later appear in *Wuthering Heights*.

Brontë Family Juvenilia

Wherever her few, brief travels took her, Emily always worked her way back to Haworth to continue her creative work begun in childhood. The bulk of this work consisted of the fantasy Gondal saga she and Anne wrote together, writings that make up part of what has come to be known as the Brontë siblings' juvenilia.

The well-documented impetus for the Brontë children's creative writings occurred in June 1826, when Emily was eight years old. Having returned from a trip, Reverend Brontë presented Branwell with a gift of twelve wooden soldiers. Each of the Brontë sisters immediately claimed a soldier as her own, named him, and began spinning tales in which all of the soldiers could act, eventually developing them into plays that the children acted out for themselves and others.

These creative stories made the leap from oral entertainments to the written page in 1829, when the Brontë children sent their soldier characters on an imaginary journey to explore the northwest coast of Africa. As the story developed, Branwell created a journal, documenting the characters' exploits. The book was proportioned to the size of the toy soldiers and written in minute handwriting to suggest that the soldiers had written the entries themselves. It was stitched together and had a paper cover. In addition to personal accounts of travels, the journal also included poetry, scientific articles, and illustrations. Charlotte eventually contributed to the journal as well, and later Anne and Emily would create their own series. Over a hundred volumes of the tiny books exist today, some of which remain on display at Haworth Parsonage, which is preserved as a national monument and tourist attraction in England.

That the Brontë children were devoted to their creative literary pursuits is clear. In fact, Norman Sherry writes,

> They would seem to have lived more in their imaginary kingdoms of Angria and Gondal than in the real world. . . . But the actual world, particularly the political and literary events of the time, played its part in their games, as their choice of heroes shows. Wellington and his two sons, Napoleon, Leigh Hunt, Walter Scott, Lord Bentinck, Christopher North, editor for *Blackwoods Magazine* [which Branwell's first soldier journal was modeled after], all appear in their fictional worlds.[5]

THE GONDAL SAGA

The soldiers' African adventure occupied the collective Brontë imagination for two years before Charlotte left home to attend Roe Head School in 1831. At this time, Emily and Anne left the continuation of the African stories (later known as the Angrian stories) to Branwell, so that they could create an adventure of their own. This adventure became the Gondal saga, taking place on the imaginary island of Gondal in the North Pacific. Emily became especially devoted to the project and continued her Gondal writings, both poetry and prose, into adulthood. In fact, Benvenuto writes, "At least 117 of her 195 poems are definitely or very probably Gondal poems, and they exist in several manuscript and printed sources."[4]

Brontë scholars have studied the Gondal saga for its expansive plot developments and recurring themes, but due to lost portions of the manuscript, obscure ideas in Emily's poems, creative leaps in the chronology, and multiple points of view, they do not always come to the same conclusions. We do know, however, that like the wooden soldier stories of their earlier years, in Gondal, Anne and Emily created a very specific, imaginative world of kingdoms and kings, discoveries and conquests, wars and revolutions, and loves and infidelities. In the world of Gondal, Benvenuto writes of Emily's poems, "Brontë's characters are both heroic, larger than life, and flawed or limited, and their image for us shifts as we see them from their own point of view and from that of their victims and enemies."[5]

THE GONDAL INFLUENCE IN *WUTHERING HEIGHTS*

Some critics have suggested that Brontë's characters, emotions, and themes in *Wuthering Heights* bear similarities to those of the Gondal saga. Edward Chitham, for example, believes that Emily's poetry (much of which, as noted, was Gondal related) and her early creative experiences directly influenced *Wuthering Heights*. "The themes, like Heathcliff," Chitham says, "were 'always, always' in Emily's mind," and the book itself is a "chart of the inner country of her dreams."[6]

Chitham notes that the structure of *Wuthering Heights* is oral in that the novel relies on the narratives of Nelly Dean and Mr. Lockwood. It is shaped, then, by the same tradition (family storytelling and the fictions she playacted with her siblings) that helped develop Emily's creative sensibilities. The Gondal saga, we should recall, was first an oral exchange between Emily and Anne before it was written down. In light of Emily's preoccupation with the saga, it seems fitting that her only novel should reflect the tradition that influenced her early work.

In addition to sharing elements of the same literary traditions, *Wuthering Heights* and the Gondal saga also contain similar themes. For instance, Chitham explains that the theme of duality appears in both works as well as in her non-Gondal poems. In *Wuthering Heights*, the theme of duality is apparent first in the characters of Heathcliff and Catherine, and again in Hareton and Cathy. These character pairs are each "two parts of a whole," Chitham says. Emily's "tendency to see things in pairs" is also expressed in poems in the Gondal series. Chitham notes that in two contrasting Gondal poems, we also get a sense that two children "are two sides of the same being,"[7] just as Emily's important *Wuthering Heights* characters are.

Other themes represented in both the Gondal poems and *Wuthering Heights* include: infidelity, the appearance of mysterious children, haunted landscapes, and nature. When considering the natural landscape of her work, it is important to remember that Emily Brontë was not well traveled and that her fictional settings most often reflect her own surroundings. Clearly, the moors are important in *Wuthering Heights*, but Emily's natural environment is expressed in Gondal as well. Chitham writes:

> Emily's absorption in it [nature] is the chief cause of her moving her fictional world to a Yorkshire climate. In fact, her close geographical knowledge of the "lone green lane" suggests that she transfers Yorkshire features lock, stock, and barrel to Gondal, though this should not be taken to mean that the lane is necessarily the path from Haworth to the moors, as is often suggested.[8]

BRIEF FREEDOM AT HOME

For two years (1836–1837) after returning home from her Roe Head School experience, Emily divided her time between educating herself at home, contributing to the upkeep of Haworth, and working on the Gondal saga. While all accounts of her life at this time suggest that she was happy during this period, the family was in need of additional financial support. Charlotte was earning a small wage, but Branwell Brontë, Emily's older brother, had failed as a student at the Royal Academy and could not be counted on to earn money for the family. Feeling pressure to contribute to the family, Emily gave up her idyllic lifestyle at Haworth at age nineteen to become a governess at Law Hill School in Halifax.

Although Emily was able to produce a number of poems during her stint as a governess, suggesting that her creative activities were less stifled at Law Hill than they had been at Roe Head, she was unable to adjust to the rigors of teaching. Biographers note that Emily viewed the school as a dungeon or prison, and she was not particularly fond of her students or the socializing expected of someone in her position. She was not made ill by the experience, and she completed a full term of service, but she returned home after six months nonetheless, with more fondness in her heart for the school dog than her students.

Next, Emily entered into what is noted by Brontë scholars as her most creative period. Between 1838 and 1842, for example, from age twenty to twenty-four, Brontë wrote over half of her surviving poems. With regard to the literal content of this work, Benvenuto writes that although Brontë's life was essentially uneventful during this period, her inner creativity flourished. The Gondal saga was growing, he says, and she "created new speakers for her poems, expanded her themes of captivity and prisonhood, and identified herself with the figure of the wanderer and exile."[9]

PLANS FOR A SCHOOL OF THEIR OWN

While continuing to write poetry, Brontë also made an effort to progress in her education and make plans for the future. In 1841 the Brontë sisters began discussing plans to open their own school so that they could remain together and provide additional financial security for the family. Before embarking on this venture, Charlotte encouraged Emily to travel with her to attend a girl's school in Brussels, the Pensionnat Héger, where they would study languages.

Charlotte and Emily remained reserved at school in Brussels, and Emily had to work much harder than Charlotte to keep up with the work. After nine months, however, both had progressed sufficiently for the Hégers to offer them student teacher positions. Charlotte was expected to teach English, and Emily was to give piano lessons, experience that would be beneficial when they returned to England to open their own school. None of these plans came to fruition, however. In November 1842 Elizabeth Branwell, the girls' aunt, died at Haworth. Charlotte and Emily returned to England to care for their father and the parsonage, though Charlotte soon returned to Brussels to complete her education.

Later, in 1844, the Brontë sisters attempted to establish the school they had dreamed of three years earlier. When no students responded to their advertisement, Emily was the first to lose interest in the project. A small inheritance left by Aunt Branwell was enough to give the girls their first taste of financial security, and Emily was eager to devote herself to her own creative work again. Although none of the Brontë sisters ever maintained any longevity in their various teaching positions, it is interesting to note that their strong feelings about the value of education, teachers, and governesses often are reflected in their novels. For example, in *Wuthering Heights,* Sherry says, "The idea of the need for education, discipline, and control is present. Cathy and Heathcliff 'both promised fair to grow up as rude as savages; the young master being entirely negligent how they behaved, and what they did.'"[10]

THE WRITER AT HOME

Home again, where she would remain for the rest of her life, Emily Brontë immersed herself in domestic life and her writ-

ing. With renewed devotion to her creative work, Brontë began seriously to revise her poetry and organize her poems
into two manuscripts in 1844. The first manuscript, book A,
contained Emily's personal poems, poems that related to her
own experiences and views of the world. Manuscript B contained her Gondal poems. This was her imaginative work,
which contained the Gondalan fantasy world and the fictional characters that had preoccupied her imagination since
childhood. Edward Chitham writes of the two manuscripts
that we can

> note the small, concentrated, intellectual cast of the writing,
> so angular and so erratically spaced. Each word is dashed off
> at speed, but there are pauses for reflection. There is power in
> the darkness of the ink, economy in the tiny sheets of paper
> used. Letters and words are blotted and blurred, as if the com-
> munication is self-communication. There are wavering lines
> to divide each poem from its neighbor in the A and B manu-
> scripts. The bare minimum is written by this restless, over-
> taxed pen.[11]

Emily Brontë did not write her poems, nor go to the trouble of organizing them into the two manuscripts, with an eye
toward publication. In her mind, her creative work was personal, her way of balancing her outer world with her inner,
imaginative one. In 1845, however, Charlotte discovered
Emily's poetry, much to Emily's dismay, and was impressed
by what she read. Emily felt that Charlotte had intruded into
her private world, but after much urging, Charlotte per-
suaded her to publish a selection of her poems, along with
her own and Anne's, in a single-volume work. The Brontës
spent their own money (a considerable amount in the
1800s—thirty-five pounds) to pay the costs of publication.

Aware of the existing prejudice against women writers
and thus feeling that they would not be treated fairly nor
taken seriously if they divulged their work was by women,
the sisters chose pseudonyms that were ambiguous in gender. Charlotte later explained this choice in her "Biographical Notice" in the second editions of *Wuthering Heights* and
Anne's *The Tenant of Wildfell Hall:*

> Averse to personal publicity, we veiled our own names under
> those of Currer, Ellis, and Acton Bell; the ambiguous choice
> being dictated by a sort of conscientious scruple at assuming
> Christian names positively masculine, while we did not like to
> declare ourselves women, because—without at that time sus-
> pecting that our mode of writing and thinking was not what is
> called "feminine"—we had a vague impression that au-
> thoresses are liable to be looked on with prejudice; we had

noticed how critics sometimes use for their chastisement the weapon of personality, and for their reward, a flattery which is not true praise.[12]

The work, *Poems by Currer, Ellis and Acton Bell*, was published in 1846 by Aylott and Jones publishers, when Emily was twenty-eight. Two copies sold.

THE NEED FOR PSEUDONYMS

The Brontës' suspicions were well founded. In the literary climate of the Brontës' time, women were not respected as serious writers. While lending libraries had a need for books that made ripe the possibility of literary success, women were bound by their duties in the home in the eyes of the male public, not to mention the critics. Indeed, Sherry notes that one George Lewes wrote at the time, "Does it never strike these delightful creatures that their little fingers were made to be kissed not to be inked? . . . Are there no stockings to darn, no purses to make, no braces to embroider? *My* idea of a perfect woman is one who can write but won't."[13]

BRONTË'S PUBLISHED POETRY

While a large proportion of Emily's poetry is from the Gondal saga, the poems she published in 1846 with her sisters were her personal, less fantastically imaginative poems. Reflective and lyrical, these poems express many of the same themes of the Gondal poems but in a more realistic realm. Sherry describes her work as "taking in the themes of tragic separations and exiles, treachery, death, and rejection of the temporal and petty values of the world."[14] Using the ballad form and eighteenth-century hymns as structural influences in her work, Brontë rarely presented much that was innovative for her time in her poetry, but she used these forms to her advantage. She is praised for her simple language and use of symbol, and her ideas, "though not original," Sherry says, "are notable for the intensity with which they are held."[15]

Today Brontë's poetry is read primarily by scholars and remains unknown to the average reader. Her poetry is rarely included in anthologies of Victorian literature, and when her poems are studied, Benvenuto says, it is "mostly as foreshadowing of *Wuthering Heights*, as autobiography, or as clues to the nebulous Gondal puzzle."[16] Benvenuto suggests that one possible reason for the general lack of appreciation for Brontë's poetry is that her work was so unlike that of her contemporaries. She did not concern herself with the events or conflicts of her day, despite Victorians' growing concerns over the industrial revolution and Darwinism. Instead, her poems "question and affirm the nature and validity of her imaginative vision." [17] Brontë's poetry, then, is not the work of public prophecy, but a private journey toward self-fulfillment.

BITTERSWEET PUBLICATION SUCCESS

Emily Brontë completed *Wuthering Heights* in 1846; the manuscript was accepted for publication under her pseudonym, Ellis Bell, the same year. Anne's *Agnes Grey* and Charlotte's *Jane Eyre* were published within a few months of Emily's novel in 1847. Although the sisters were pleased to see their novels in print and to have the chance to become known authors, their first publication experience was not altogether positive.

Because of the immediate success of Charlotte's *Jane Eyre*, Thomas Newby, Emily and Anne's publisher, helped fuel the rumor that the Bell books were all written by Currer Bell, Charlotte's pseudonym. In 1848, when Anne's second book, *The Tenant of Wildfell Hall*, was published, Newby blatantly marketed the book in America as Charlotte's. Publishers' confusion over authorship of the Bell novels became so great that Anne and Charlotte were compelled to travel to London to expose their pseudonyms and prove their separate identities. Emily, however, adamantly wished her true identity to remain secret.

THE RECEPTION OF *WUTHERING HEIGHTS*

All of the critical reviews of the first edition of *Wuthering Heights* were written not only under the assumption that Ellis Bell was male, but also under the firm belief that no woman could ever write such a shocking, masculine novel. Although the novel sold out its first edition and did receive some critical acclaim for its "power" and the literary promise of its author, most reviews were hostile. Critics were irritated and baffled by the book; they described it as, among other things, eccentric, depraved, corrupt, cruel, and lacking in social or moral value.

In the critics' eyes, Nicola Thompson writes, the novel failed to "replicate middle-class ideals." The reviews, she writes, show an "ambivalence, an overwhelming sense of confusion and frustration mixed with admiration, as reviewers struggle to reconcile *Wuthering Heights* with novelistic conventions." [18] These Victorian conventions included the need for a moral, a purpose to the writing that pleased readers and refined the ordinary world, and most importantly, characters that were themselves moral and well behaved. *Wuthering Heights* has few of these.

EMILY'S DEATH AND THE "UNVEILING OF ELLIS BELL"

Emily Brontë did not live to see the publication of the second edition of her novel. Branwell Brontë, a drunkard and opium addict at the time of his death, succumbed to consumption on September 24, 1848. It was at his funeral that Emily caught the severe cold and cough that led to inflammation in her lungs. Refusing to rest in bed or to accept medical treatment, she died less than three months later on December 19, 1848, in the parlor at Haworth. When Emily died, the literary world still did not know she was the author of *Wuthering Heights*. Charlotte changed that.

A little more than a year later, Charlotte wrote her "Biographical Notice" for the second edition of *Wuthering Heights* to clear up questions of authorship. Her reasons for writing can be seen as twofold. First is her genuine concern that Emily be given credit for her work. However, Charlotte was also concerned with distancing herself from its authorship, as Currer Bell had been criticized by some reviewers for trying to exploit the success of *Jane Eyre* by hastily publishing an earlier, inferior novel.

While Charlotte tried to clear up the authorial confusion surrounding the novel, she also caused additional controversy. Some critics, convinced that a man wrote *Wuthering Heights*, refused to accept Emily as author and suggested rather that Branwell Brontë had dictated it to her. The other result of Charlotte's notice was that reviewers now read the novel in a new light.

Learning that Ellis Bell was a woman, reviewers changed their attitude about *Wuthering Heights*. Thompson explains that

> When *Wuthering Heights* was thought to be by a male Ellis Bell, it was shocking, but at the same time was praised for its masculine-associated qualities—power, originality, the way in which it differentiated itself from "effeminate" works. Its problem was that it went too far in this direction: ironically, it was too "male," and perhaps therefore not suited for a "feminized" reading public.[19]

Now, they read it as a love story, a "feminine romance," and where before they had only seen masculinity, now they found evidence of female authorship within the text. Thompson writes that the tone of the reviews changed as well from one of bewilderment to confidence, even to condescension.

THE EFFECT OF CHARLOTTE'S PREFACE TO *WUTHERING HEIGHTS*

In her preface to the novel, also written for the second edition, Charlotte, who was working on building her own image as a respectable Victorian writer, has been described as again trying to distance herself from her sister's work. The preface suggests ambivalence toward the book's merit; she especially questions the moral character of Heathcliff and indeed whether he should have been at all.

Charlotte also felt the need to explain Emily's background in an attempt, perhaps, to excuse the coarse elements of the novel. To this end, Thompson writes that Charlotte creates

> an image of Emily as, in some ways, a stereotype of the ideal Victorian woman; passive, nun-like, innocent, domestic, and ignorant of the outside world. In other ways she depicts her as so strange that she cannot be held subject to Victorian ideas about social conventions: she is a child-like mystic, with a passionate attachment to the natural world.[20]

Just as the notice of authorship affected, for better or worse, the new reviews of *Wuthering Heights*, so does Charlotte's portrayal of Emily in the preface. Rather than focus on the novel itself, reviewers now read it filtered through the biographical information Charlotte provides. Critics now "take Charlotte Brontë's lead in responding to and echoing [her] comments about Emily's innocence, the isolation and eccentricity of her lifestyle, and the effects of the region on her work," says Thompson, and this new view of Emily's life increased sympathy for the novel and "excused the author from normal standards of literary and female propriety."[21]

EMILY LIVES ON

Emily Brontë wrote very little after the publication of *Wuthering Heights* the year before her death. We have only two poems from that period and no physical evidence that she wrote any other pieces of fiction. Emily retreated into herself more and more during that last year. Some critics suggest this retreat was due in part to anger she felt toward Charlotte for revealing Ellis Bell's gender to publishers in London. Others suggest she lost her old passion for work after her novel was published, or that unidentified early stages of her illness simply prevented her from working with her usual dedication. Certainly all Brontë scholars have wondered at one time or another what Emily would have written had she lived, and what impact her work would have had on us as she polished her craft and thought more deeply about, and perhaps ventured beyond, her common themes.

Although she attained no fame as a writer in her lifetime, Emily Brontë is recognized among the renowned Victorian writers today. While her contemporaries did not fully appreciate *Wuthering Heights*, at least one person close to Emily—Charlotte—felt a sense of its power, its potential to transcend Victorian society and survive as it does today. The strength of the novel is not unlike the strength of its author in her last days as described by Charlotte:

> She made haste to leave us. Yet, while physically she perished, mentally she grew stronger than we had yet known her. Day by day, when I saw with what a front she met suffering, I looked on her with an anguish of wonder and love. I have seen nothing like it; but indeed, I have never seen her parallel in anything. Stronger than a man, simpler than a child, her nature stood alone.[22]

NOTES

1. Edward Chitham, *A Life of Emily Brontë*. Oxford: Basil Blackwell, 1987, p. 65.
2. Richard Benvenuto, *Emily Brontë*. Boston: Twayne, 1982, p. 9.
3. Norman Sherry, *Literary Critiques: Charlotte and Emily Brontë*. New York: Arco, 1970, p. 14.
4. Benvenuto, *Emily Brontë*, p. 25.
5. Benvenuto, *Emily Brontë*, p. 39.
6. Chitham, *A Life of Emily Brontë*, p. 199.
7. Chitham, *A Life of Emily Brontë*, p. 206.
8. Chitham, *A Life of Emily Brontë*, pp. 207–208.
9. Benvenuto, *Emily Brontë*, p. 15.
10. Sherry, *Literary Critiques*, p. 35.
11. Chitham, *A Life of Emily Brontë*, p. 248.
12. Charlotte Brontë, "Biographical Notice of Ellis and Acton Bell," *Wuthering Heights*. New York: Random House, 1943, p. vi.
13. Quoted in Sherry, *Literary Critiques*, p. 36.
14. Sherry, *Literary Critiques*, p. 101.
15. Sherry, *Literary Critiques*, p. 110.
16. Benvenuto, *Emily Brontë*, p. 41.
17. Benvenuto, *Emily Brontë*, p. 42.
18. Nicola Thompson, "The Unveiling of Ellis Bell: Gender

and the Reception of *Wuthering Heights*." *Women's Studies*, vol. 24, no. 4, March 1995, p. 343.

19. Thompson,"The Unveiling of Ellis Bell," p. 346.
20. Thompson, "The Unveiling of Ellis Bell," p. 346.
21. Thompson,"The Unveiling of Ellis Bell," p. 348.
22. Brontë, "Biographical Notice of Ellis and Acton Bell," p. ix.

CHAPTER 1

The Inhabitants of *Wuthering Heights*

READINGS ON
WUTHERING HEIGHTS

Heathcliff Is Both Tyrant and Victim

Graham Holderness

As Heathcliff changes throughout Brontë's novel, readers alternately hate and sympathize with him. Graham Holderness, an educator at University College of Swansea in Wales and author of *D.H. Lawrence: History, Ideology, and Fiction* and *Shakespeare's History*, explores this love/hate relationship with Heathcliff and suggests that both emotions are justifiable. Although Heathcliff becomes a tyrant, bent on revenge after years of humiliation at Wuthering Heights, he can also be seen as an obsessive and bereaved outsider—a sympathetic victim.

Heathcliff is really the central problem of *Wuthering Heights*: our valuation of him determines our sense of what the novel is about. If you think about it, it would perhaps be more orthodox to regard Edgar Linton—who has all the conventional requirements—as the hero, and Heathcliff as the villain of the piece. Heathcliff never does anything virtuous or noble in the conventional sense: his story is a long list of morally reprehensible actions. Are we supposed to see Heathcliff (in the words of the *Examiner*, 8 January 1848) as 'an incarnation of evil qualities; implacable hate, ingratitude, falsehood, selfishness, and revenge'—and despise him? Or are we supposed to sympathize with him in his obsessive pursuit of love and then revenge? . . .

In the 1840s critics were divided on the subject of the book's 'morality'. Those who thought the book *immoral* seem to have assumed that Emily Brontë wanted us to admire the obviously immoral Heathcliff. Those who thought it moral assumed that she wanted us to judge him. These two ways of looking at him aren't the only ones, but they are the most common. How then are we supposed to see Heathcliff?

Reprinted from *Open Guides to Literature: "Wuthering Heights,"* by Graham Holderness. Copyright © 1985 by Graham Holderness. Used by permission of Open University Press.

HEATHCLIFF THE TYRANT

If we look at what he actually does in the novel, in the abstract, it's a pretty disgusting performance. This process is attempted in a critical article by Philip Drew called 'Charlotte Brontë as a critic of *Wuthering Heights*'. Drew thinks that Charlotte's judgement on Heathcliff was correct: 'Heathcliff . . . never once swerving in his arrow-straight course to perdition'. She solved the problem of orientation within the moral world of the novel—the problem of knowing what we should think, what we should feel, how we should value—by reading it firmly within a known and recognizable moral system. As Drew writes:

> Charlotte's assessment of Heathcliff depends on a recognition of his superhuman villainy, whereas modern critics . . . usually choose to minimise or justify Heathcliff's consistent delight in malice in order to elevate him to the status of a hero.

Drew then provides a long catalogue or charge-sheet of Heathcliff's actual misdemeanours. Catherine calls him 'a pitiless, wolvish man', and this assessment, Drew argues, is borne out by his actions. When he returns to Wuthering Heights as an adult, he immediately begins to lead Hindley Earnshaw to perdition; he courts Isabella Linton not out of love but desire for revenge; he breaks up the marriage between Catherine and Edgar; he has a fight with Hindley in which he knocks him down and kicks him; there is evidence that he murders Hindley; he degrades and perverts Hareton; he treats his own son Linton with great cruelty, trapping the second Cathy into marrying him, and finally letting him die without calling a doctor. All these actions are perpetrated with a savage and voracious appetite for inflicting cruelty. Drew sums up:

> His whole career is one of calculated malice: during this time he does not perform one good or kindly action, and continually expresses his hatred of all other characters. So extreme is his malevolence that one might expect him to impress critics as a grotesque villain like Quilp in *The Old Curiosity Shop*.

Some readers respond sympathetically to this hostile view of Heathcliff. Others feel that there is much more to admire both in Heathcliff's character and in what he represents: the figure of quenchless love, enormous suffering, irrepressible pride and resolute refusal to submit to circumstances or fate. Philip Drew's own critical approach should perhaps also be subjected to some interrogation: do we really respond to the actions of a fictional character in exactly the same way as we would to such actions performed by a real person? If Heathcliff does not impress readers as a grotesque villain like Quilp, does that not indicate some profound difference of artistic effect? You must of course reach your own decision about Heathcliff, as about every other aspect of the novel: to assist you I will offer two alternative ways of thinking about Heathcliff himself, before proceeding to consider him in relation to Catherine. . . .

THE UNWANTED GYPSY

The following passage describes Heathcliff's initiation into Wuthering Heights and into the Earnshaw family: . . .

> They entirely refused to have it [Heathcliff] in bed with them, or even in their room, and I had no more sense, so I put it on the landing of the stairs, hoping it might be gone on the morrow. By chance, or else attracted by hearing his voice, it crept to Mr Earnshaw's door and there he found it on quitting his chamber. Inquiries were made as to how it got there; I was obliged to confess, and in recompense for my cowardice and inhumanity was sent out of the house.

> This was Heathcliff's first introduction to the family: on coming back a few days afterwards, for I did not consider my banishment perpetual, I found that they had christened him 'Heathcliff'; it was the name of a son who died in childhood, and it has served him ever since, both for Christian and surname.

> Miss Cathy and he were now very thick; but Hindley hated him, and to say the truth I did the same; and we plagued and went on with him shamefully, for I wasn't reasonable enough to feel my injustice, and the mistress never put in a word on his behalf, when she saw him wronged.

> He seemed a sullen, patient child; hardened, perhaps to ill-treatment: he would stand Hindley's blows without winking or shedding a tear, and my pinches moved him only to draw in a breath and open his eyes, as if he had hurt himself by accident and nobody was to blame. This endurance made old Earnshaw furious when he discovered his son persecuting the poor, fatherless child, as he called him. He took to Heathcliff strangely, believing all he said (for that matter, he said precious little, and generally the truth), and petting him up far above Cathy, who was too mischievous and wayward for a favourite.

> So, from the very beginning, he bred bad feeling in the house; and at Mrs Earnshaw's death, which happened in less than two years after, the young master had learnt to regard his father as an oppressor rather than a friend, and Heathcliff as a usurper of his parent's affections and his privileges, and he grew bitter with brooding over these injuries.

The most striking aspect of the family's reaction to Heathcliff is its immediate and instinctive hostility. Nelly consistently refers to the child as 'it', denying Heathcliff any human status. He is not only treated with callous indifference, he is subjected to active and gratuitous cruelty. Consider the succession of verbs denoting ill-treatment in the three paragraphs beginning 'Miss Cathy and he were now very thick'—*hated, plagued, wronged, hardened, persecuting*; all summed up in the single word *injustice*.

The 'bad feeling' Heathcliff arouses seems entirely disproportionate to what he is and does. Is it that this close-knit family structure, with its long ancestral past, is threatened and challenged by the arrival of an outsider, a stranger who has no proper place in the family? One who simply requires acceptance, without claim or justification? Evidently the 'bad feeling' arises from within the family itself, rather than from Heathcliff.

The 'gipsy brat' old Mr Earnshaw brings home with him has neither name nor status, property nor possessions. He emerges from that darkness which is the *outside* of the tightly-knit family system: an outsider who *tests* the family by introducing an alien element into a jealously-guarded system of parental and filial relations, of inheritance and possession. 'You must e'en take it as a gift from God', says old Mr Earnshaw 'though it's as dark as if it came from the devil'. Heathcliff can be either gift or threat, by virtue of his single passive demand, to be loved: Catherine takes the opportunity of loving him, and thereby disturbs the family's equilibrium. Hindley sees Heathcliff as a rival for his father's affections and his own position as heir, a potential disrupter of the ancient lineage; and accordingly hates him. Heathcliff here is not the instigator but the recipient of violence: violence which his arrival has provoked in that defensive, exclusive family unit. The violence, then, is latent in the family structure, and provoked by an individual who expects to be treated as an equal.

HEATHCLIFF'S REVENGE

Naturally, however, these experiences have their effect on him: we begin to see emerging a representative pattern of victimization begetting violence, injustice provoking resentment. Heathcliff doesn't remain a victim all his life: he deliberately resolves to free himself from the humiliation of oppression by attaining for himself the status of an oppressor. His plan of revenge, carefully laid and executed, is to revenge himself on Hindley and the Lintons by two methods: oppressing and exploiting their children, Hareton and Linton Heathcliff, in precisely the same way that Hindley and Edgar oppressed and exploited Heathcliff; and by expropriating their lands and possessions and seizing them himself. Heathcliff makes the identification between himself and Hareton very clear:

> Now, my bonny lad, you are *mine*! And we'll see if one tree won't grow as crooked as another, with the same wind to twist it!

I think most readers find it difficult to sympathize with Heathcliff's actions after he returns, even though we may recognize in them a 'rough moral justice'. It would surely be impossible to sympathize wholly with him, since our initial sympathy went to him as a victim of oppression—and we very soon see that in order to secure his revenge he has become an oppressor himself:

> The tyrant grinds down his slaves—and they don't turn against him, they crush those beneath them. You are welcome to torture me to death for your amusement, only, allow me to amuse myself a little in the same style—And refrain from insult as much as you are able. Having levelled my palace, don't erect a hovel and complacently admire your own charity in giving me that for a home.

But if Heathcliff, the novel's only candidate for the status of 'hero', loses our sympathy in respect of his actions, where does it go? Do we begin to take sides with the Lintons, or is a vacuum of sympathy set up in the novel? . . .

HEATHCLIFF'S MORAL INSIGHT

In Chapter 10 Nelly conceives an intense dislike for Heathcliff. At the beginning of Chapter 11 the direction of her feelings guides our own—towards the child Hareton, who is now in the position Heathcliff occupied formerly. Hindley and Hareton are now victims of a tyrant: we feel sympathy for them, not the tyrant himself.

Hareton develops from this point into a very important element in the novel. The development of the relationship between him and Cathy is a continuation of the Catherine–Heathcliff relationship. . . .

Why does Heathcliff avoid striking Cathy?

He had his hand in her hair; Hareton attempted to release the locks, entreating him not to hurt her that once. His black eyes flashed, he seemed ready to tear Catherine in pieces, and I was just worked up to risk coming to the rescue, when of a sudden his fingers relaxed, he shifted his grasp from her head to her arm, and gazed intently in her face—Then, he drew his hand over his eyes, stood a moment to collect himself apparently, and turning anew to Catherine, said with assumed calmness, 'You must learn to avoid putting me in a passion, or I shall really murder you, some time!'

Because, seeing Hareton and Cathy unite in love and comradeship against brutal and tyrannical oppression, he recognizes himself and Catherine as they were together, rebelling against an oppressive regime. Heathcliff has come to see the emptiness of his triumph: he has recognized that Hareton is himself; Catherine's daughter, Catherine. He has achieved the same moral insight into them as we have into Heathcliff himself in the early stages of the novel.

Catherine Earnshaw: Mother and Daughter

Linda Gold

In this Freudian analysis of the "internal landscape" of Brontë's novel, Linda Gold, an instructor at the Packer Collegiate Institute in Brooklyn, New York, identifies aspects of id, ego, and superego spanning the generations to shape the personality development of the novel's two Catherines, mother and daughter. Gold also defines the personalities of other key characters in an attempt to show the motivation behind the elder Catherine's destructive divided loyalties and her eventual emotional decline and death. Likewise, the younger Catherine's decisions are influenced by the personalities of those surrounding her. While maintaining aspects of her mother's fragmented and untamed nature, she is nonetheless successful at entering into what her mother could not: a placid domestic life.

The landscape depicted in *Wuthering Heights* is not only an external one; it is internal as well.

The maturation of Catherine Earnshaw resembles the development of the personality described by Sigmund Freud. The first generation and its intense struggles evoke the early conflicts in the emergent personality. The intense symbiosis of Catherine, Heathcliff, and Linton suggests an interaction within the personality of the id, the ego, and the superego.[1]

---

1. The id, according to Freud, is that basic, primal, unrestrained part of the personality in which resides the human being's most basic drives. The id is motivated by the pleasure principle, since the id aims at almost all times to seek pleasure and to avoid pain. . . . It is impossible, however, for the id to achieve its ends without interaction with the external environment. Hence—the ego, that part of the personality which engages in reality testing. The id announces its primitive needs and the ego intercedes with the external environment, modifying the pleasure principle with the reality principle, forcing the id to postpone release of its energy until gratification can reasonably be achieved. The third part of the personality, the superego, is concerned with the innumerable "shoulds" of civilization. It is the voice of parents, of the church, of social convention.

Excerpted from Linda Gold, "Catherine Earnshaw: Mother and Daughter," *English Journal*, vol. 74, no. 3 (March 1985), pp. 68–73. Copyright 1985 by the National Council of Teachers of English. Reprinted by permission.

Not only are the lives of the three characters inextricably bound, but ultimately they are buried in what Heathcliff envisions as a single coffin. . . . The three here literally merge into one.

As the story suggests, no one's mother approves of Heathcliff; he is the id personified. Although everything about his character bespeaks his wildness and distance from civilization, he enters the Earnshaw home not from without but from within: Earnshaw draws the boy Heathcliff from under his own greatcoat. Nelly Dean describes the first encounter of the "wild gipsy brat" with the Earnshaws: "When it was on its feet, it only stared round, and repeated over and over some gibberish that nobody could understand." The origins and parentage of this bestial child are a mystery. When Lockwood encounters the adult Heathcliff at Wuthering Heights, Heathcliff has become one with a setting as primitive and remote from civilization as he is. All of its inhabitants, canine and human, are snarling, unrestrained, and exemplary of the word "wuthering"—"descriptive of the atmospheric tumult to which its station is exposed in stormy weather." Like the id, Heathcliff remains primitive and unmodified by the passage of time. As a child, he runs barefoot and dirty through the moors; later, at Catherine's deaths he "groaned in a sudden paroxysm of ungovernable passion . . . he dashed his head against the knotted trunk; and, lifting up his eyes, howled, not like a man, but like a savage beast." When he hears from Lockwood of Catherine's spectral appearance at the window of Wuthering Heights, he wrenches open the window and bursts into an "uncontrollable passion of tears."

Linton, on the other hand, is consummately civilized. His home is Thrushcross Grange, whose name and appearance suggest gentility and cultivation. Edgar is fair-haired, polite, correct, wealthy, and gentlemanly. It is he who, as the conscience, forces Catherine to choose between her husband and Heathcliff, and who, cooly, from the cerebral retreat of the library, severs ties with his sister Isabella when she disobeys his dictates. Edgar never shirks his duty or tolerates dereliction in others.

Then, there is Catherine, who is the ego. Yet Catherine is female, and the reality she faces offers her few genuine choices. There is little outlet for her primal desires; there is a single culturally-endorsed position—that of wife. When this female ego confronts and tests reality, she must confront also her lack of power and freedom in this male world.

CATHERINE'S DESTRUCTIVE DIVIDED SELF

[According to Freud,] the ego, that part of the personality which faces the world, must be male. And so Catherine, Brontë's female child, first attempts to emerge through her male children, Edgar Linton and Heathcliff. She must attempt to live through men if she is to live at all. Catherine resolves this dilemma through narcissistic identification with two men.

That Catherine identifies with Heathcliff is clear. As children, they are nearly inseparable, running together on the moors and mocking together Joseph's superstitious and tedious pieties. As Catherine says to Nelly Dean, "Nelly, I *am* Heathcliff—he's always, always in my mind, not as a pleasure, any more than I am always a pleasure to myself, but as my own being."

But she also identifies with Edgar Linton. It is the visit to Thrushcross Grange and Catherine's resulting injury which ends her earlier exclusive identification with Heathcliff. For this visit, marked by a debilitating wound and the resulting ministrations of the Lintons, coincides with Catherine's emergence as a woman, an emergence which requires that she attempt to take her place in a world which so rigidly defines her. After a five-week sojourn at the Grange, she returns to the Heights, having transformed herself into a lady. . . .

After her decision to marry Linton, Catherine describes her feelings for the two men to Nelly:

> My love for Linton is like the foliage in the woods. Time will change it, I'm aware, as winter changes the trees. My love for Heathcliff resembles the eternal rocks beneath—a source of little visible delight, but necessary.

Here Catherine's description captures the primal and timeless quality of the id as well as its relationship to the rest of the personality. The id is not "visible" or conscious. Linton, like civilization, is more apparent, as trees can be seen more readily than underlying rock. Yet it is the id which is the constant necessary basis for the personality.

It is not Catherine's intention to fragment her personality: she aims at synthesis. Although she feels that it would "degrade" her to marry Heathcliff or to surrender totally to her instinctual self, she continues to see Heathcliff as "more myself than I am." Her intention, therefore, is to maintain her union with both men, and to use Linton's position to help Heathcliff "rise." However, this attempt is frustrated by Heathcliff's flight. Catherine is successful as Linton's wife as long as Heathcliff, with whom she has identified her primal urges, is absent. Nelly describes Catherine during this period as "infinitely better than I dared expect." Yet this calm is seen as temporary and a denial of Catherine's true nature. . . .

When Heathcliff returns, so does the conflict within Catherine. But, because the conflict is not external to her, the reconciliation she attempts is impossible. Freud describes such a dilemma in *The Ego and the Id.*

> If they (the ego's object identifications) obtain the upper hand and become too numerous, unduly powerful, and incompatible with each other, a pathological outcome will not be far off.

If the conflict between diverse identifications becomes too acute, the ego loses control. Because Catherine has split apart her personality through her identification with these two men, no synthesis is possible. The only possible resolution is Catherine's death. . . .

Catherine vainly hopes that she can achieve the integration of her divided self, but this hope is as futile as her effort to crush the two hands into one. As she despairs of wholeness, she cries to Nelly, "I'll try to break their hearts by breaking my own," suggesting that to her the three hearts are one. When Edgar, ever the moralizer, forces what is in effect a dissolution of her own personality by offering his ultimatum: "It is impossible for you to be my friend and his at the same time; and I absolutely require to know which you choose," Catherine is driven into a frenzy. . . .

On her deathbed, the agitated Catherine begins to rend apart a pillow, as she is being rent apart, and to identify the feathers of the wild birds which fill it, as if she recognizes the wildness that lies beneath every thin covering of civilization.

Catherine seeks death as a release from the unendurable tension created by her inability to synthesize the fragmented segments of her personality, a fragmentation necessitated by the constricting environment which provides no outlet for her psychic energy. Shortly before she dies, she confides to Nelly:

> Oh, I wish I were out of doors—I wish I were a girl again, half savage, and hardy and free . . . and laughing at injuries, not madding under them. Why am I so changed? . . . I'm sure I should be myself were I once among the heather on those hills . . . Open the window again wide, fasten it open!

CATHERINE EARNSHAW IS DESTROYED
BY HER PASSIONATE NATURE

Norman Sherry notes that after making the "impossible choice" of marrying Edgar Linton over Heathcliff, Catherine finds that she must repress her wild and passionate self. Unable to recapture the freedom and happiness of her childhood years, she is driven to self-destruction.

In making the decision to marry Edgar, [Catherine] did not realise fully that it meant cutting herself off not only from Heathcliff, but from the wildness and freedom she had enjoyed as a child. Her true nature is wild and rough and passionate, but, in face of the 'invariable courtesy' she experiences at the Grange, she conceals her true nature, and 'adopts a double character'. Thus, she is ladylike with the Lintons, but reverts to her natural self at the Heights. It is this natural self which Linton glimpses when she nips Nelly, shakes Hareton, and slaps Linton himself, so that he says to her, 'You've made me afraid and ashamed of you.'

The scene of her delirium is very important. Heathcliff's return has aroused that true nature which the life at Thrushcross has allowed to lie buried. . . . Through her own action she has chosen the controlled, but wealthy man. Now she finds herself in what she thinks of as a hostile environment—Edgar, Isabella, Nelly, all disliking or fearing her, wanting her out of the way so that things can return to normal. Then, reverting to Heathcliff, she remembers how he set a trap over a lapwing's nest so that the parent could not feed its young—'we saw its nest in the winter, full of little skeletons'. In her delirium, she sees clearly what Heathcliff is—the unnatural being who comes between parent and child, who disrupts the course of nature with deliberate and senseless cruelty. But 'I made him promise he'd never shoot a lapwing after that'. This reflects her former control over Heathcliff. But a moment later, she doubts that control—'Did he shoot my lapwings, Nelly?' Then she sees Nelly as an old witch who wants to cause mischief—which in part she does. Finally, she imagines herself removed from the Heights as a child, without any introductory process, and set down into the Grange, and envisages her misery. This is the way she would have felt had she been taken from Wuthering Heights and Heathcliff as a child, and this is, fundamentally, the source of her unhappiness now. For this reason, she wants to return to the Heights and childhood—the period of her freedom and happiness. For this reason also, she sees her only means of being reunited with Heathcliff as being through death.

Norman Sherry, *Literary Critiques: Charlotte and Emily Brontë.* New York: Arco, 1970, pp. 124–26.

When Nelly refuses, claiming she won't "give Catherine her death," of cold, Catherine replies, "I'm not helpless yet, I'll open it myself."

And Catherine does release herself, through death. . . .

THE NEW CATHERINE

But the novel, as students persist in pointing out, does not end with Catherine's death. The youthful and passionate Catherine Earnshaw both dies and lives transformed in the person of her daughter and namesake, Catherine Linton. Therefore, it can be argued that the entire saga of two generations of Earnshaws, Lintons, and Heathcliffs is the odyssey of a single personality, parts of which are "male" and parts of which are "female." This personality begins with Catherine Earnshaw and ends with Catherine Linton Heathcliff Earnshaw, or a Catherine Earnshaw who has incorporated and reconciled those elements represented by Linton (superego) and Heathcliff (id). According to Freud, when the id is frustrated in the attainment of its desires by contact with reality, the ego provides a series of substitutions; this energy may be sublimated or directed toward a more socially acceptable object. Energy within the personality, like physical energy, is not destroyed, but transformed. What Catherine cannot achieve—freedom from tension, reconciliation of the opposing forces in her nature—is finally achieved by the daughter. For, in one sense, Catherine does not die at all, for shortly before her death, she gives birth to another Catherine, Catherine Linton, a partial synthesis of the opposing forces within her personality.

Catherine achieves her "spring through the window," her return to girlhood, both through her death and through young Catherine who is born as Catherine dies "having never recovered sufficient consciousness to miss Heathcliff or to know Edgar." As Catherine lies in newfound repose, the infant "wails out of life." Catherine's conflict is both reborn and transformed in the infant who possesses Catherine's vitality and spirit tempered by the Lintons' gentleness. . . .

Through her two marriages, young Catherine achieves the serenity her mother was denied, for marriage is a melding of male and female into one, a reconciliation of male and female within the personality. Her first marriage is to the repellent Linton Heathcliff, whom Nelly describes as "the worst tempered bit of a sickly slip that ever struggled into his teens.". . .

He combines the Lintons' constitutional weakness, described by Nelly as "listless apathy," with Heathcliff's infantile self-absorption and hysterical emotional dependency. Despite his questionable appeal, Catherine is drawn to him and he to her, and like her mother, defies Edgar Linton to maintain their relationship. When Nelly warns young Catherine that Edgar Linton has ordered that the friendship between Catherine and Heathcliff must not be revived, the girl replies defiantly, "It has been revived." This love contains further echoes of the struggles of the previous generation. . . .

Young Catherine, by doing what her mother did not do, by marrying Heathcliff, in a sense, validates her mother's fear of degradation. Marriage at the Heights becomes a thralldom surpassing that of thralldom at the Grange. Catherine, desperate at the news of Edgar's dying but imprisoned by Heathcliff and his son, leaps from a window at the Heights to reunite herself with that part of herself dying with her father, as her mother once leapt through a window at the Grange. . . .

LIFE WITH HARETON: A NEW DOMESTICATION

After Edgar's death, Catherine returns to Wuthering Heights, to be "buried alive." The Catherine Lockwood discovers and addresses as "Mrs. Heathcliff" is sullen, cruel and a bit depraved. On her face is an expression which hovers between "scorn and a kind of desperation." Accused by the sanctimonious Joseph of heading "raight to t' divil, like (her) mother before (her)," the "little witch" practices the black art on the red cow. But Wuthering Heights and a life as "Mrs. Heathcliff" is not Catherine's final destination. For the H., which "might be" for Heathcliff, might also be for Hareton.

After the deaths of Linton Heathcliff and Heathcliff, Hareton's cultivation and consequent ascendence begin. With Catherine's marriage to Hareton Earnshaw the reconciliation of conflicting elements is furthered. For Hareton is to Catherine and Heathcliff what young Catherine is to the elder Catherine and Edgar Linton: a harmonious synthesis of opposing forces. Hareton undoubtedly resembles and is allied with Heathcliff throughout the novel. Heathcliff unwittingly rescues the toddler Hareton after Hareton is tossed from the stairwell by Hindley. During Nelly's first encounter with Hareton after Catherine's marriage, the child sits at the crossroads between the two houses and extols Heathcliff's maniacal torment of Hindley. As a young man, Hareton admires and imitates the actions of Heathcliff: both prefer activities like demonstrations of poor table manners and the hanging of dogs. And the sullen "brute" Lockwood encounters is strongly reminiscent of the boy Heathcliff. But not only does Heathcliff see himself in Hareton, he sees Catherine, who is Hareton's aunt, as well. "But when I look for his father in his face, I see *her* more everyday." Through the marriage of these two, Catherine becomes Catherine Earnshaw again; Hareton and Catherine (H. and C.) begin a placid domestic life at Thrushcross Grange, having tamed those primal elements which caused such depths of torment and such heights of ecstasy.

But not entirely. For one part of Catherine's untamed nature, that part which leapt through the window at her death, remains. This part is represented by the plaintive wailing of the unsatisfied Catherine Linton at the window of Wuthering Heights; Catherine Linton (and Lockwood is puzzled by the spectre's identification of herself as "Catherine Linton" and not "Catherine Earnshaw") attempts to gain access to that fragment of herself imprisoned within the house, that fragment of herself represented by her daughter, then Catherine Heathcliff. This part is also represented by Heathcliff, whose spirit leaps also from the window to roam the moors again. . . .

Paired with Hareton, Catherine the daughter is contentedly acculterated but pallid; indeed, few readers remember that she occupies the novel at all. Paired with Heathcliff, Catherine the mother, unfettered, passionate, utterly memorable, discovers that although heaven does not seem to be her home, neither can she fully occupy the earth. The novel's ending both offers and withholds a resolution: Catherine the woman remains fragmented, spirit and body, wanton and wife, male and female. Catherine's anguished desire to be herself expresses a uniquely female suffering: nowhere does she exist as herself, whole and entire.

Mr. Lockwood

George J. Worth

University of Kansas English instructor George J.
Worth writes that critics often disagree about Mr.
Lockwood's role in *Wuthering Heights*. Worth contends that Brontë intends Lockwood to be a distinct
and well-defined character whose gregarious nature,
sentimentality, and clumsy wordiness lend insight
into important events of the novel and other characters. Lockwood, Worth explains, is an ironic character,
and he is the novel's only comic figure. He expels
much energy in characterizing himself as a "victim of
passion," but compared with the "superhuman love"
of Heathcliff and Cathy, his fantasy affair amounts to
nothing. He declares himself a misanthrope, but the
characters of *Wuthering Heights*, and readers too, see
him for his sociable, curious self.

The character of Mr. Lockwood, one of the two narrators of
Wuthering Heights (the one through whose consciousness all
the events of the plot are ostensibly filtered) has been the subject of much critical disparagement and disagreement. Even if
it is granted that Emily Brontë's elaborate manner of placing
her material before the reader is not impossibly cumbersome,
Lockwood himself is generally considered something of a
prig and a dullard. Dorothy Van Ghent, for instance, refers to
him as "the effete, almost epicene Lockwood," and similarly
slighting epithets abound in the sizable critical literature that
has grown up around *Wuthering Heights*.

But critics differ regarding the precise role which Lockwood plays in the novel. At one extreme, there is Mark
Schorer, who sees the figure of Lockwood, the symbol of
conventional emotion, as one of the chief means by which
Emily Brontë's theme—unconsciously on her part, he implies—is brought home to the reader. At the other, May Sin-
clair affirms that Lockwood is not, properly speaking, a

Reprinted from George J. Worth, "Emily Brontë's Mr. Lockwood," *Nineteenth-Century
Fiction*, vol. 12, no. 4, pp. 315–20. Copyright © 1957 by The Regents of the University
of California. Used by permission of the University of California Press.

character at all: he is purposely left a vague sketch by Emily Brontë, for "he is a mere looker-on." The middle road is taken by Melvin R. Watson, who regards Lockwood as a character in his own right but without the thematic significance Mr. Schorer reads into him: he is "an ordinary person from the outside world" with whom the reader can identify himself as Mr. Lockwood and become immersed in the strange atmosphere of the Heights, Thrushcross Grange, and the bleak moors that lie between.

Although there has been no scarcity of commentaries on Lockwood's personality nor of attempts to define his relationship to the material he is supposed to narrate, no critic as far as I know has taken a searching look at the manner in which Emily Brontë characterizes Lockwood or drawn from this the appropriate conclusions regarding his function in the novel. It is my thesis that she *did* intend him to stand as a clearly defined figure, and that she indicated to us, by implication rather than by explicit statement, in what light we are to regard him.

Lockwood is endowed by Miss Brontë with three leading traits, each important in helping him to fulfil his role in the novel: an ill-disguised gregariousness, a sentimental (as opposed to a passionate) view of life and love, and a clumsy and tactless garrulity.

LOCKWOOD'S MISTAKEN MISANTHROPY

He represents himself in the opening paragraphs of *Wuthering Heights* as a misanthrope—he has rented a house on the desolate Yorkshire moors, he says, because he regards the region as a "perfect misanthropist's heaven"—and some critics have taken his view of himself at face value. But what are the facts? He calls on his neighbor and landlord "as soon as possible after my arrival"; treated with surliness and contempt by Heathcliff on this first visit, he nevertheless resolves to come again the next day; having weakened in his determination to return, he seizes on a flimsy pretext—the servant girl is cleaning his study—to trudge four miles in threatening weather to enjoy once again the pleasantries of Heathcliff and the other inmates of the Heights; and after his return from this unfortunate second expedition, bored, lonely, and ill, he relentlessly pumps Mrs. Dean for information about Wuthering Heights, its inhabitants and their history, thereby getting for us the story of the novel.

Obviously, had Lockwood been the misanthrope he claimed to be, he would have shunned all intercourse with Heathcliff and Nelly and there could have been no novel, at least not in its present form. Emily Brontë had to create him as a sociable and more than normally curious character. If he had been genuinely contemptuous of everything outside himself, would he have bothered on his second visit to the Heights to look into Cathy's Bible, thus precipitating the nightmare-vision which introduces us to the supernatural element in *Wuthering Heights?*

Why, then, does Emily Brontë invest Lockwood with this veneer of misanthropy which so quickly peels away under the scrutiny of even a moderately observant reader? Clearly, to furnish an appropriate vantage point from which to observe, and an appropriate standard with which to compare, Heathcliff's true misanthropy. Lockwood, deluded about his own character, insists on seeing Heathcliff as something he is not, and the change in his opinion, when it comes, is as painful as it is illuminating. Since we identify ourselves temporarily with the narrator, the truth about Heathcliff's fierce nature dawns on us gradually—although probably not quite so gradually as it does on him. And Lockwood's spurious scorn for mankind and yearning for isolation furnish a pale background against which Heathcliff's violent misanthropy, when revealed, blazes with unnatural brightness.

It is interesting to observe how Lockwood's estimate of Heathcliff changes. In the first paragraph of the novel he calls him, with a wide-eyed enthusiasm that is typical of him at this stage, "A capital fellow!"

"He little imagined," he goes on, "how my heart warmed towards him when I beheld his black eyes withdraw so suspiciously under their brows, as I rode up, and when his fingers sheltered themselves, with a jealous resolution, still further up in his waistcoat, as I announced my name!" Two of a kind, obviously! Later in the opening chapter, Lockwood indulges in some analysis of the character of his taciturn host, a task for which he considers himself uniquely qualified by virtue of their similar outlook on life; needless to say, his analysis is hopelessly wide of the mark.

> Possibly, some people might suspect him of a degree of underbred pride; I have a sympathetic chord within that tells me it is nothing of the sort: I know, by instinct, his reserve springs from an aversion to showy displays of feeling—to

manifestations of mutual kindliness. He'll love and hate equally under cover, and esteem it a species of impertinence to be loved or hated again.

(But Lockwood is not an utter fool: he adds, "No, I'm running on too fast: I bestow my own attributes over liberally on him.") By the end of the first call he pays him, Lockwood confesses to some bewilderment concerning Heathcliff's character–"It is astonishing how sociable I feel myself when compared with him"—and after he has seen Heathcliff's savagery in its full force during his second visit to Wuthering Heights, even the vapid Lockwood can remain under no illusions regarding Heathcliff's nature or the identity in feeling between them.

A VICTIM OF PASSION?

Why has Lockwood sequestered himself in the remote wilds of Yorkshire? He regards himself as a man cruelly disappointed in love, and presumably he hopes to nurse his wounds and recover his equanimity in isolation. But his view of himself as a victim of passion is no more admissible than the role of misanthrope he insists on assuming, as is obvious from the paragraph in which he fatuously sets forth the history of his romance.

> While enjoining a month of fine weather at the seacoast, I was thrown into the company of a most fascinating creature: a real goddess in my eyes, as long as she took no notice of me. I "never told my love" vocally; still, if looks have language, the merest idiot might have guessed I was over head and ears: she understood me at last, and looked a return—the sweetest of all imaginable looks. And what did I do? I confess it with shame— shrunk icily into myself, like a snail; at every glance retired colder and farther; till finally the poor innocent was led to doubt her own senses, and, overwhelmed with confusion at her supposed mistake, persuaded her mamma to decamp. By this curious turn of disposition I have gained the reputation of deliberate heartlessness; how undeserved, I alone can appreciate.

This absurdly stunted love affair and Lockwood's occasional daydreams about the pleasures of a possible romance with Catherine seem to be the extent of his capacity to feel passion—an atrophied capacity to which the superhuman love of Heathcliff and Cathy furnishes a violent contrast. Indeed, all the unruly emotions in which *Wuthering Heights* abounds seem much more strange when viewed from the vantage point of the humdrum sentimentalist who gives us the story.

In showing us Lockwood's indomitable inclination to be sociable and his tamely conventional outlook on the events of the story, Emily Brontë employs considerable irony. She lets Lockwood characterize himself, and then helps us to realize, by letting us witness his character in action, that he is not really like that at all. The incongruity between the way a man regards himself and the way he is regarded by others is, of course, a perennial source of comedy, and Lockwood is the only genuinely comic figure in *Wuthering Heights*.

ALWAYS TALKING

Lockwood's third key threat, his bumbling talkativeness, also helps him to carry out his function in the novel. In addition to branding him even more completely as a good-natured buffoon, his well-meant but inane chatter serves to draw out, more successfully than a more discreet character could have done, Heathcliff and the other members of his menage, thus furnishing the reader with valuable information about them. For instance, in chapter ii, Lockwood's dogged efforts to be ingratiating give Emily Brontë an opportunity to display Hareton and Catherine at their most churlish, and his persistent questioning of Heathcliff drags out of him an account of the relationship between these strange people. His imprudent babbling to Heathcliff of his dream also helps move the story along.

> If the little fiend had got in at the window, she probably would have strangled me! . . . I'm not going to endure the persecutions of your hospitable ancestors again. Was not the Reverend Jabes Branderham akin to you on the mother's side? And that minx, Catherine Linton, or Earnshaw, or however she was called—she must have been a changeling—wicked little soul! She told me she had been walking the earth those twenty years: a just punishment for her mortal transgressions, I've no doubt!

It is in response to this outburst that the impassioned Heathcliff, a few moments later, tears open the bedroom window and tearfully beseeches the spirit of Cathy to come to him—the first concrete indication we have that he is moved by something more than mortal impulses.

As previous critics have recognized, Lockwood is an ordinary observant man, the representative of the great body of ordinary readers, viewing an extraordinary situation much as any of us might view it. But he is more than this: he is a distinct character—a character with comic overtones—in his own right, whom Emily Brontë deliberately fashioned as she did to serve as a useful source of information and an often unconscious commentator on the series of events around which she built her novel.

Nelly Dean: The Storyteller

Bonamy Dobrée

Nelly Dean is one of two narrators of *Wuthering Heights*, perhaps the more important of the two. Bonamy Dobrée, author of the introduction to the 1953 Collins Classics edition of *Wuthering Heights*, writes that Brontë's choice of narrators lends authenticity to her text. While Lockwood's role as narrator remains a mechanical one, Dean, because she witnesses the most crucial incidents of the novel, is involved at its core. In a position to influence the actions of major characters, she not only reports on the events around her but becomes part of their "emotional texture."

It is universally acknowledged that *Wuthering Heights* is a great work of art, in itself an experience: it colours our view of what life is about. It is of enormous interest to ask ourselves, not "How did this astonishing thing happen?"—one cannot track down genius in that way—but rather "By what means did Emily Brontë produce her effect?" We may be quite sure that this is not the lucky result of untutored genius flinging itself haphazard at the task. The actors live in as small an enclosed world as they do in any of Ibsen's later plays, and the book has all the tension of a drama, together with the final effect of drama rather than of the novel: that is, we do not drop into a muse when we have finished it: we feel exhilaration. This is the achieved result of long brooding on the theme until the imagination encounters the symbols which will embody it: and then of the imagination concentrating powerfully on the means of making these living symbols real for other people. That is where the intellectual problem must emerge with the intuitional creation.

Emily Brontë had had practice in the Gondal romance or

Reprinted from Bonamy Dobrée, Introduction to *Wuthering Heights*, by Emily Brontë, Collins Classics (London: HarperCollins, 1953), courtesy of the publisher.

epic, and in the other writings conducted by all four Brontë children; so there is nothing slack or amateurish about the conception of this book. The relationships of the people, the working out of the dates of the events, the fitting in of the various conflicts, all are mechanically perfect; and what is more, Emily Brontë had learnt, so that she might apply it here, the complicated law of inheritance which prevailed, not when she wrote, but at the time of the story she was telling. She must, we see, have been able to live in a vivid state of actuality with her people while she was creating them. Not that this is uncommon, for after all, this is what normally constitutes inspiration; what is rare is the faculty of intense visual imagination which she shared with her elder sister, a sense of vision so strong that she can impart it to us incidentally, almost: she never has to reassure herself of the existence of her people by describing them minutely.

TWO NARRATORS ARE BETTER THAN ONE

What may seem nearly as astonishing when considering a first novel, written before much had been said about the craft of fiction, is that Emily Brontë seems to have been acutely alive to the problem of presenting her material, of making her vision tell upon the page. She must certainly have pondered the technical side of novel writing, and it surely was deliberately that she chose the two narrators as vehicles for her tale. It might have been better, we may think, if she had taken up the position of the all-seeing creator, the method usually adopted by her predecessors and contemporaries when they were not using the autobiographical convention clearly unsuitable here: but whereas the omniscient method is well enough where there is no temptation to disbelieve what you are told, as, say, in Jane Austen's novels which deal with the normal, here, with so wild a story, the method would have exposed its greatest flaw, namely that there is nothing to guarantee for the reader that he is being told the truth. Yet it was essential to Emily Brontë's purpose that you should believe it, wholly and utterly accept it: so she gave the story into the hands of two narrators, each of whom can say, "This is true; I was there; this is what happened." We know then that the story is authentic.

But how was Emily Brontë to find someone who would always be, who could plausibly be, there, just when it was absolutely necessary for her to be present? She had recourse to the confidential servant, brought up with the children of the family, necessarily involved in all their affairs. But then, how can an uneducated woman have the knowledge—of complex circumstances, of outrageous sentiments, of words, of artful story-telling—to satisfy the requirements of a story at that level, to be a trustworthy witness? Emily Brontë was quite aware of the difficulty: almost as soon as Ellen Dean begins to take up the tale, she reassures her temporary master: "I have undergone sharp discipline, which has taught me wisdom: and then, I have read more than you would fancy, Mr. Lockwood. . . ." It is true, on examination, that only a very highly cultured, literary woman, could speak and discuss as Nelly does at the end of the book: but by that time verisimilitude has ceased to matter—to anyone for whom the means of communication offered by novels has any validity at all.

Yet—a further complication, which might have been disastrous—it is not to us, but to Lockwood, that she tells her story. Lockwood even repeats to us what Nelly says somebody else told her was uttered by yet another person, as when we know what the Lintons remarked when the Wuthering Heights children broke in upon them. All their sayings are reported verbatim, and this undoubtedly introduces a certain clumsiness. Every method involves its own risks, exacts even some payment: the question is, can the author, by proper handling of the method, keep up so great a pressure on our consciousness, We too are at the moment reassured: and soon we cease to our recipience, as to justify the price paid in verisimilitude? It must be confessed that once or twice, in the very middle of the book, our belief wavers. What, we ask, was the "good authority" which apprised Dr. Kenneth of there being something afoot between Heathcliff and Isabella? And how, soon afterwards, did Nelly Dean get Isabella's letter, and why was such an unlikely epistle addressed to her at all? Just for a moment, then, the pressure slackens: but it is for a moment only that we feel uneasiness. Such is the force and passion of the prose, the speed of the narrative, that we soon accept again.

For though the story seems thus unnecessarily involved, it does not seem so in the reading, for the scenes are dramatized without our noticing it; the "he said"s are left out whenever dramatic actuality is demanded. Moreover Nelly is introduced as narrator only after we have had what is, so to speak, a first-hand glimpse of the atrocious agony of feeling which gives the book its power. For the deep emotions in

action are presented to us, not in retrospect as they ultimately must be with a narrator, but as a violent scene in
which the first narrator, Lockwood, is willy-nilly caught up.
We do not have to wait for Nelly and her contemporaries,
Cathy and Hindley and Heathcliff to become responsible
adults, but are plunged straightway into the maelstrom of
feelings which direct the story. Today the method is the ordinary one—it was not so much the routine in 1846—a
scene to begin with, then a retrospect, then a summary, with
the tale going on: even so, in this book, the first scene is very
long, and the retrospect occupies nearly all the rest of the
book: the summary and the continuing tale are almost in the
nature of an epilogue. All the same the effect is achieved.

INVOLVEMENT VERSUS DETACHMENT

Nelly is brilliantly thought out and executed; nothing more
clearly reveals the power of a novelist than making the vehicle of communication really convey the intuition, and not
merely relate events. Since she is the confidante of so many
people, the story does not suffer from the usual defect of the
narrator method, that of seeing people from only one point
of view: Heathcliff, for example, we see not only through her
eyes, but through the first Catherine's, when she tells Isabella what Heathcliff is like; through the unlucky Linton
Heathcliff's, when Nelly sees him shrink in terror from his
father; and even through the devoted eyes (an amazing
touch of art) of Hareton Earnshaw. Lockwood too is ad-
mirably conceived as a narrator; he never has to be drawn
into the emotional development; he is external and detached, though he is not unnecessary to the story. For he is
all unconsciously an agent, and we realize at the end that it
was his visitation by the ghost of Cathy (if we choose to regard his nightmare as such) that precipitated Heathcliff's final crisis. Apart from that, however, he is outside the story.
His role is to add convincing evidence to what Nelly tells us
through him, since he has no need to lie, no subconscious
urge to conceal, reveal, or justify. He clinches Nelly's statements: he confirms for us the ghastly truth of what she tells.
It is through this quite disinterested person that from the
very beginning we feel the tension of the whole story.

So much for what we might call the purely mechanical
side; there is more to be noticed. We see that since Nelly is so
often "there" we do not miss any of the dramatic possibilities

when the great scenes occur, but we have to realize further that this can happen only because she is the kind of person Emily Brontë chose to make her. It is not simply that as a family servant she identifies herself with the family and is personally involved in all that happens: it is that her own feelings are part of the drama; it is through her passion that we feel it. One might instance this particularly from her anger with Cathy at her fatal fit of temper when Heathcliff is turned out of Thrushcross. Moreover, she has enough of the peasant in her to be able to sit and brood over the past; she re-lives it, one feels, over and over again; it is all arranged (or re-arranged) in her mind with perfect clarity. So that when she tells any part of the story she does actually re-live it, and the drama is vividly present to her, not dimly seen, not sophisticated, as it nearly always is in a narrator's retrospect. Again, for Emily Brontë's purpose, she is just educated enough to understand what is happening, but not so educated as to be anything but acceptant. There is no scepticism in her. Someone more analytical could not have told about Heathcliff's last visionary days, if only, for one thing, that Heathcliff could not have talked as he did to any other kind of person.

Nelly, then, is not a mere mechanical vehicle; she is part of the emotional texture, not simply chorus to the tragic scene in company with the hideous Joseph. She is there at every one of the crucial moments except the tremendous opening one where Lockwood sees Heathcliff frantically imploring Cathy's ghost to come in. It is to her that Cathy says: "I *am* Heathcliff"; it is to her that Heathcliff says: "My soul's bliss kills my body, but doesn't satisfy itself." It is she who is present at the last despairing interview between the two eternal lovers, where at once both Heaven seems to open and Hell to gape. Nevertheless all the time Emily Brontë is in control—perhaps Ellen Dean was her sheet anchor in this respect. But then she can be broken away from. Lockwood, the detached—or almost detached—observer comes back to report to us directly; and how ingeniously, we note, Emily Brontë had sent him away for a few months, so that Nelly can tell him the rest of the story quickly. The tale thus gathers speed towards the end, and the gap enables a sane love, not the "monomania" of Heathcliff or the tormented possession of the elder Catherine, to break in upon the fire-purged horror, so that the story can be dovetailed, as it were, into our daily life lived at the normal intensity.

CHAPTER 2

The Art of
the Novel

READINGS ON
WUTHERING HEIGHTS

Brontë Controls Her Readers' Sympathies

Larry S. Champion

Many critics, conceding the "literal importance" of the character of Heathcliff, say he is not a true protagonist but a tyrannical villain—even a vampire. However, Larry S. Champion, an associate professor of English at North Carolina State University, disagrees. Champion believes that Brontë aptly controls her readers' sympathies towards Heathcliff by populating the moors with a variety of imperfect people who do not grow by the novel's end. Joseph remains steeped in Christian hypocrisy, the meddlesome Nelly acts only in self-interest, and Edgar lacks all ability to forgive. Heathcliff, it seems, is the only character who truly redeems himself by eventually renouncing his violent ways.

While it would be naive to expect all readers to react similarly to Heathcliff, my contention is that an examination of Emily Brontë's attitude toward her central figure, as it can be glossed from the narrative itself and of the techniques by which she directs and controls the reader's sympathy, will provide a fresh focus on her apparent intentions concerning this enigmatic character. Such an approach is all the more pertinent when one considers that the characterization of Heathcliff is essentially static. There is no internal development; instead there is a careful manipulation of the reader's attitude toward the character, what he is and what he represents in the world of the novel. . . .

As Arnold Kettle has so effectively argued, Heathcliff is a vivid personality, born not in the pages of Byron but in the Liverpool slums. Any attempts, on the one hand, to abstract his passions of love and vindictive hatred are surely amiss. Certainly the character may be symbolic of elemental aspects

Excerpted from Larry S. Champion, "Heathcliff: A Study in Authorial Technique," *Ball State University Forum*, vol. 9, no. 2 (Spring 1968), pp. 19–25. Copyright © 1968 by Ball State University. Reprinted by permission of the publisher.

of the human personality but this is not to say his importance is to be found only in the complex fabric of cosmological and psychiatric imagery or that he does not exist as a realistic fictional personage in his own right. On the other hand, to maintain that the reader does not, to a degree at least, sympathize with Heathcliff and envision him as the dominant character of the novel is to neglect the apparent intentions of the author. Indeed, Brontë's narrative is only as real and as credible as this malcontent, for her story is Heathcliff—his mistreatment, his methodic retaliation and the attendant effects upon the inhabitants of Wuthering Heights and Thrushcross Grange, and his death and metaphysical reunion with Catherine. Even though our conventional morality is shaken, we find ourselves in sympathy with him, sometimes almost in spite of ourselves, simply because we are made to feel his superiority to those around him. When the technique by which the author develops this situation is closely considered, one realizes how concerned she is that the relationship between reader and Heathcliff be a compatible one.

WHERE ARE THE CHRISTIANS?

Brontë, in the first place, creates a fictional world in which Heathcliff's actions can be not merely tolerated, but literally condoned. This she accomplishes by carefully dechristianizing the atmosphere of the novel. Obviously a sympathetic portrayal of Heathcliff's crass scheme of revenge would be impossible were his action to be measured by any meaningful standard of Christian conduct within the surrounding characters. To take diabolic advantage of Hindley's drunken stupor at gambling, to deprive the younger Catherine of seeing her dying father, to terrorize his sickly son into a fatuous proposal of marriage—these and other such acts are unchristian in every sense of the word. Yet, in order to prevent the reader's moral condemnation of these actions within the context of the narrative, Brontë depicts Heathcliff in a world in which Christianity is both hypocritical and inept. In effect, she virtually makes us despise Christianity as it is portrayed in the novel and in turn respect Heathcliff for his natural strength of character, however perverse, and his candor in articulating his intentions and his unswerving dedication to their accomplishment. To this end, the atmosphere of the novel is of primary importance in establishing the perspective through which the reader evaluates the central character.

This attitude, hostile to Christianity, is established early—in the expository action of Lockwood's visit to Wuthering Heights, specifically in Lockwood's first dream in Catherine's childhood bed. The weary dreamer is escorted to a religious meeting by Joseph, Heathcliff's servant, and is "condemned to hear all out," a pious discourse divided into 490 parts. When Parson Jabes Branderham begins to preach on the "First of the Seventy-First," Lockwood, able to endure no more, rises in protest. Then, in the manner reflective of vicious Puritanical condemnation, Branderham pronounces him the unpardonable sinner: "Thou art the man. . . . Brethren, execute upon him the judgment written!". . .

JOSEPH'S HYPOCRISY

The cruel fervor of the incident suggests the more sordid aspects of Calvinistic determinism twisted to man's own ends—the pharisaic judgment of man upon man and the perpetration of sadistic violence in the name of one's concept of God. Once set, the mood is maintained throughout the narrative, primarily through the actions of the servant Joseph, who constantly spouts the Scripture though his own life is sordid, mean, and unchristian. The reader is first aware of the servant's surly incivility when, mumbling "The Lord help us," Joseph wilfully disobeys his master's orders to come up from the cellar during Lockwood's visit; similarly he refuses to open the door for Lockwood on his return visit the next day; he incites the dog to a brutal attack upon the visitor at his departure. Later, when Isabella is brought to Wuthering Heights as Heathcliff's wife, he sneers at her contemptuously, asserting that he will never deign to call her his mistress. And, the hypocrisy of his invoking the name of God and of quoting Scripture contorted to his own perversity is unbounded. To the possibility of Heathcliff's death on the storm-riddled night of his disappearance, Joseph chants, "Thank Hivin for all! All warks togither for gooid tuh them as is chozzen, and picked aht froo th' rubbidge." To the younger Catherine, whom he dislikes intensely, he spouts; "Yah'll niver mend yer ill ways; bud goa raight to th' divil, like yer mother afore ye! . . . May the Laord deliver us from evil!" To the singing of carols, he retorts "It's a blazing shaime ut Aw cannut oppen t' Blessed Book, bud yah set up glories tuh Sattan, un'all t' flaysome wickednesses ut iver wer born intuh t' warld! . . . O, Lord, judge 'em, fur they's norther law nur justice amand wer rullers." Through all his mouthings of God, his homilies, and the recitations of the catechism which he forces upon the children, the reader is forced to recognize him for what he is—to use Nelly's words—"the wearisomest self-righteous pharisee that ever ransacked a Bible to rake the promises to himself, and fling the curses on his neighbors."

NELLY'S MEDDLING

Another character, whom the reader places within the Christian frame of reference is the primary narrator, Nelly Dean. She is what J.K. Mathison has termed a "normal," "moral," "practical" person. Yet, here again, though more subtly, Brontë forces the reader's final evaluation of her and the view of life which she represents to be a critical one. She professes to "have undergone sharp discipline which has taught [her] wisdom," yet, on his first night in the Earnshaw home, she callously places Heathcliff "on the landing of the stairs, hoping it might be gone on the morrow." She claims the Christian kinship of brotherly love, but she is totally undisturbed by the cough of Francis, Hindley's wife, disdainfully refusing to offer her sympathy unless Francis, the "foreigner," "takes to her first." More than once she admits to disliking Catherine intensely, openly relishing "the opportunity to mortify her vanity." Indeed, Nelly does better than that; she virtually precipitates Catherine's death by withholding from Edgar the seriousness of her illness and the fact that Catherine had gone without food and water for three days and nights. Too, her fidelity to her master, Edgar, is questionable. Not only does she agree to arrange a clandestine meeting between Heathcliff and the distraught Catherine, but later, specifically against Edgar's command, she allows the younger Catherine to visit Linton periodically, thereby developing that confused sympathy and pity later mistaken for love. James Hafley is no doubt correct in concluding that Nelly's actions are always motivated by self-interest, that she is constantly striving to manipulate others to improve her social status. Although the reader is slow to recognize her true character because she is relating most of the story herself and obviously is attempting to display her actions in the best light, Nelly, in the final analysis, is recognized as a gossiper and meddler. . . .

EDGAR'S FURY

Edgar, described by Nelly as "one who trusts God," offers yet another example of atrophied Christianity. In fact, he is the most striking single illustration, for it is precisely his refusal to trust and to forgive which—more than the actions of any other single individual—is responsible for the savagery of Heathcliff's revenge. After his three-year absence, Heathcliff admits to Catherine that his intentions have been to settle his score with Hindley, but asserts that "your welcome has put these things quite out of my mind." Edgar, however, refuses to offer the civilities which would have provided an atmosphere in which to suppress a vindictive nature. From the

NO ONE IS "NICE" IN THIS BOOK

V.S. Pritchett praises Brontë for writing a refreshing Victorian novel that does not moralize and for treating passion as a "natural pattern of life." Pritchett recognizes the hateful passions of Brontë's characters in inhabitants of England's isolated Yorkshire moorland and dales.

I have been reading *Wuthering Heights* again, after 20 years, a novel which is often regarded as poetical, mystical and fabulous. No people like Heathcliff and Catherine, it is said, ever existed. *Wuthering Heights* is indeed a poetical novel; but when I was reading it, it seemed to me the most realistic statement about the Yorkshire people of the isolated moorland and dales that I have ever read. I am a southerner; but I spent a good deal of my childhood in those Northern cottages and I recognise the implacable, belligerent people of Emily Brontë's novel at once. The trap used to pick you up at the branch line station and in a few miles you were on the moors, the wind standing against you like an enemy, the moorland drizzle making wraiths over the endless scene, and the birds whimpering in cries of farewell, like parting ghosts. Austere, empty, ominous were the earth and sky, and the air was fiercer and more violent than in the South. The occasional small stone houses stuck up like forests, the people themselves seemed, to a southerner, as stern as soldiers, and even the common sentences they spoke were so turned that, but for a quizzical glitter in the eyes of the speaker, one might have taken their words as challenge, insult or derision. I do not mean that these remote Yorkshire people were not kindly and hospitable folk; but one had not to live among them for long, before one found that their egotism was naked, their hatred unending. They seemed to revel in a hostility which they called frankness or bluntness; but which—how first moment of Heathcliff's return, Edgar is suspicious, resentful, and unforgiving. And the intensity of his passionate petulance, later his fury, reflects a genuinely bad temperament which cannot lightly be explained away as matrimonial jealousy for Catherine. She herself is led to brand her husband a spoiled child who fancies the world was made for his accommodation.

Later, shouting that Heathcliff is a "miserable, degraded character," Edgar forbids any future visits to Catherine and Thrushcross Grange.

> Your presence is a moral poison that would contaminate the most virtuous—for that cause, and to prevent worse con-

---

can I put it?—was an attempt to plant all they were, all they could be, all they represented as people, unyieldingly before you. They expected you to do the same. They despised you if you did not. They had the combative pride of clansmen and, on their lonely farms, clans they were and had been for hundreds of years. I can think of episodes in my own childhood among them which are as extraordinary as some of the things in *Wuthering Heights*; and which, at first sight, would strike the reader as examples of pitiable hatred and harshness. Often they were. But really their fierceness in criticism, the pride, and the violence of their sense of sin was the expression of a view of life which put energy and the will of man above everything else. To survive in these parts, one had to dominate and oppose.

There is no other novel in the English language like *Wuthering Heights*. It is unique first of all for its lack of psychological dismay. Never, in a novel, did so many people hate each other with such zest, such Northern zest. There is a faint, homely pretence that Nelly, the housekeeper and narrator, is a kindly, garrulous old body; but look at her. It is not concealed that she is a spy, a go-between, a secret opener of letters. . . . No conventional sentiment encases her. She is as hard as iron and takes up her station automatically in the battle. Everyone hates, no one disguises evil in this book; no one is "nice." How refreshing it is to come across a Victorian novel which does not moralise, and yet is very far from amoral. How strange, in Victorian fiction, to see passion treated as the natural pattern of life. How refreshing to see the open skirmishing of egotism, and to see life crackling like a fire through human beings; a book which *feels* human beings as they feel to themselves.

V.S. Pritchett, "Books in General," *New Statesman and Nation*, vol. 31, no. 800, June 22, 1946, p. 453.

sequences, I shall deny you, hereafter, admission into this house, and give notice, now, that I require your instant departure.

In effect, Edgar's condescending treatment of Heathcliff and the flat refusal to allow him to visit Thrushcross Grange—from one who is churchgoing, "God-fearing and God-abiding . . . [and who] displays . . . a loyal and faithful soul"—infuriate Heathcliff anew and unleash the flood of violence which might have been staunched.

This, in brief, is the author's portrayal of the dominant characters who claim themselves to be Christians. Surely, she has made no attempt systematically to attack any specific Christian doctrines, but the ultimate effect upon the reader can only be that he becomes unpleasantly aware of the perversities and hypocrisies of these self-righteous folk. And nowhere in the novel is there a mellowing of this sardonic tone. There is no mention, for example, of priests or heavenly reward at the deaths which occur in the novel. Heathcliff specifically forbids any minister to be present at his burial. While both he and Catherine frequently speak of the belief in their immortality, theirs is not the Christian heaven regarding either the spiritually meek or the morally stout. Instead they envision a continuation of the soul beyond the fetters of the mortal prison of the body. It is the firm conviction of a joyous metaphysical reunion with Catherine, not the sadistic, morbid fear of heavenly condemnation and punishment, that motivates Heathcliff's death wish in the final stages of the narrative.

In direct proportion to her ability to develop in the reader a critical attitude toward Christianity as it is described in her fictional world, Emily Brontë is able to establish and develop the reader's sympathy for Heathcliff, despite his violations of Christian morality. In short, by delineating the physical and mental superiority of Heathcliff when in conflict with Edgar, Isabella, and Hindley, she forces us to an evaluation of his personality on naturalistic grounds rather than those normally considered moral and ethical.

HEATHCLIFF, THE PROTAGONIST

Within a world devoid of both Christian charity and filial affection, we are faced with an environment in which the characters literally struggle for survival and in which Heathcliff emerges as the obvious protagonist. He is the underdog from his first introduction into the Earnshaw house, mistreated by all save Mr. Earnshaw and Catherine. The very fact that Mr. Earnshaw displays an affinity for the boy only intensifies Hindley's hatred. And this hatred reaches full maturation when Hindley becomes master of Wuthering Heights. Heathcliff is relegated to the servants' quarters and forced to work a full day in its fields; he is deprived of further education and insultingly forced into the back room when guests are in the house. Certainly, this pernicious and ruthless persecution of Heathcliff, who without means of self-defense can do nothing about it, provokes a fundamental comparison from the reader.

After Heathcliff's return, when he possesses the means of retaliation against his adversaries, the reader continues to sympathize with him, even though the revenge involves extreme measures, for the simple reason that at this moment in Brontë's fictional world he is the only character worthy of sympathy. The elder Catherine is dead, though her memory remains; indeed the reader is all the more sympathetic with Heathcliff because time and again he is reminded that the vehemence of hatred has resulted from that strange romantic agony which was the fate of their relationship. As yet, neither Hareton nor the young Cathy has favorably impressed the reader. The remaining characters serve only to enhance the image of Heathcliff. By comparison, Hindley is the greater degenerate—a slovenly alcoholic lacking self-control, nightly attempting but lacking the courage to murder Heathcliff. Both Edgar and Isabella are too fragile, delicate, and effete to merit the reader's sympathetic concern. These "children of the calm" are first introduced to the reader through the derisive scorn of Heathcliff and Catherine, who "laugh outright at the petted things" and "despise them." Nelly describes Edgar as one who "cries for momma at every turn" and "trembles if a country lad heaves his fist against him and sits at home all day for a shower of rain." Later, after his marriage to Catherine, a pale and trembling Edgar confronts Heathcliff at Thrushcross Grange, running for assistance after striking a cowardly blow. The same Linton weakness is evident in Isabella's son, who is miserably weak and subject to spasms of coughing and nosebleed.

And, for these latter characters at least, the reader is made to feel that each deserves his reward. Hindley's brutal abuse of Heathcliff justifies his misery; Isabella's lack of rational discipline in controlling her infatuation with Heathcliff, despite explicit warnings from Catherine, Nelly, and Joseph, provokes her disaster; Edgar's early incivilities to Heathcliff, his failure to understand his wife's nature, his outright refusal to forgive his sister for eloping with Heathcliff, and his complete lack of physical and moral stamina—all force the reader to consider his fate essentially just.

VIOLENCE SUBDUED

In the final pages of the novel, the growth of a sympathetic love between Cathy and Hareton and their determination to achieve happiness in spite of the gloom of their surroundings provide a final touchstone for evaluating the author's conception of Heathcliff. Although there is no basic alteration in Heathcliff's nature, the reader is at the point not only of losing sympathy for the central character but also of developing an overt antagonism for him. For no longer are his enmity and vindictiveness justified by the perverse nature of his adversaries; now his potential victims are innocent and youthful. It is precisely at this point, when sympathy for his revenge can no longer be sustained, that Heathcliff becomes passive and his violence subdued—not from any conscious change of heart but from a sense of exhaustion and a deepening obsession to find reunion with Catherine beyond the grave.

> An absurd termination to my violent exertions? I get levers and mattocks to demolish the two houses, and train myself to be capable of working like Hercules, and when everything is ready, and in my power, I find the will to lift a slate off either roof has vanished! My old enemies have not beaten me—now would be the precise time to revenge myself on their representatives—I could do it—But where is the use? . . . I have a single wish, and my whole being, and faculties are yearning to attain it.

Brontë has terminated Heathcliff's obsessive pursuit of revenge at the very moment when its continuance would evoke disapprobation from the reader.

There can be little doubt that the author has intended Heathcliff to be, not a devil or a bully or an elemental symbol, but a credible protagonist. She has carefully and methodically created an atmosphere in which sympathy for his revenge can be achieved and has so manipulated the surrounding characters and events that transfer of sympathy becomes a virtual impossibility. The result is that Heathcliff emerges as a mortal, fallible man twisted and tortured by the evil which pervades his environment. As such, like many tragic characters, he is corrupted and eventually consumed by his own passion, but at no time is he "unbelievable" or "unsympathetic."

The Action of *Wuthering Heights*

Norman Lavers

Instructor of creative writing at Western Washington State College Norman Lavers writes that the action of *Wuthering Heights* is governed by the necessity of restoring power to the Earnshaw family. All of the smaller actions of the novel, he maintains, work toward this ultimate end, and when characters have fulfilled their purpose of advancing the story along these lines, they are disposed of—conveniently, through death.

It is common, in beginning the discussion of a drama, to look for the one Action under which the various smaller actions can be subsumed, an Action which can be expressed in an infinitival phrase: e.g., To find the murderer of Laius. Let me suggest for the governing Action of *Wuthering Heights*, to which all the smaller actions of the novel contribute, the phrase, To restore to power the Earnshaw family.

A CHILD IS FOUND

As I am going to show how the smaller "actions" all lead to this ultimate end, it is proper to begin with old Earnshaw's bringing in of Heathcliff, for this is the action from which the rest of the novel's actions follow.

Is old Earnshaw a kind of Lear, in his dotage spurning his deserving children to favor the demon, the "cuckoo," who will destroy everything? I do not think so. Look at the situation at the chronological beginning of the story. The Earnshaw family is 300 years old. It is past its peak. Great strength is still there, but like the stunted firs growing at the end of the house, time has twisted it. Hindley and Catherine are the last of the line, and Hindley, old Earnshaw tells us, "was naught, and would never thrive as where he wan-

Excerpted from Norman Lavers, "The Action of *Wuthering Heights*," *The South Atlantic Quarterly*, vol. 72, no. 1, (Winter 1973), pp. 43–52. Copyright 1973, Duke University Press. Reprinted with permission.

dered." And to Catherine he says: "I cannot love thee; thou'rt worse than thy brother. . . . I doubt thy mother and I must rue that we ever reared thee!" Future events prove him accurate. There had been an earlier son, dead in childhood, named Heathcliff. Shall we suggest that old Earnshaw, on his long walking journey, reclaimed this lost child? Remember, this is a book full of magic, a descendant of the tales of the "fairish" told Emily Brontë by her old nurse. Heathcliff, the "it," the "demon," "ghoul," "goblin," nameless, without antecedents, speaking some "gibberish," is certainly from somewhere beyond. But from which beyond? "Where did he come from, the dark little thing, harboured by a good man to his bane?" Nelly wonders. Old Earnshaw, an accurate judge of his other children, suggests that we "must e'en take it as a gift of God, though it's as dark almost as if it came from the devil." From the beginning, the child is treated as one of his own children—in fact, it is treated better than the others. Earnshaw "took to Heathcliff strangely, believing all he said," Nelly tells us (and then confesses in a parenthesis, "for that matter, he said precious little, and generally the truth").

So here is the first action: Earnshaw reclaims a spiritual son. . . . Let us suggest that Earnshaw . . . was bringing in something from outside and beyond, new forces and powers to stir into his deteriorating stock, his last-ditch effort to save his ancient family from decline. Having performed this essential action, there is nothing more to keep him in this world, and a page or two later, he "began to fail. He had been active and healthy, yet his strength left him suddenly." This becomes a regular feature of the novel, for each character, having performed his action, done his best, goes from apparent health to immediate decline. The one exception is Nelly Dean, but, unlike the others, she never acts to change or improve anything. Her first action ("I put it on the landing of the stairs, hoping it might be gone on the morrow") is topical, for in all her actions her only motive is to preserve the status quo.

LIFE AND DEATH

The next significant action is Hindley's, and it exactly parallels Earnshaw's. He returns from an absence carrying with him, to everyone's surprise, a stranger: his wife, Frances. Her parallel with Heathcliff is pointed: "What she was, and where she was born he never informed us; probably she had neither money nor name to recommend her." Nameless, destitute, without antecedents—does she come from "beyond" herself? They are both morbidly concerned with death, though her striking difference from the necrophilic Heathcliff is that "she felt so afraid of dying!" But then she must return so much more quickly than Heathcliff, and she has no lover waiting for her there.

She performs her essential action—bearing Hareton—and at once from seeming health (Nelly "imagined her as little likely to die as myself") goes into immediate decline. Hindley, unable to bear the loss, loses himself in dissipation. He, it is clear, is not going to rejuvenate the family; it is Catherine's turn to act. She will marry Edgar Linton. "It would degrade me to marry Heathcliff now," she reasons, even though she loves him. But her action, like Earnshaw's action, is, in its own peculiar and regardless way, unselfish. "Nelly, I see now, you think me a selfish wretch, but, did it never strike you that if Heathcliff and I married, we should be beggars? whereas, if I marry Linton, I can aid Heathcliff to rise."

But just as Earnshaw's unselfish action in taking Heathcliff in had alienated Hindley, first banishing him from the house (to college), and then bringing him back with education and power over Heathcliff, power to revenge himself on him, so now Catherine's unselfish action banishes Heathcliff, to return with education and power to revenge himself on the others. Once more, Catherine performs her essential action—bearing Cathy—and having done so, she dies, declining rapidly from robust health.

I believe a pattern is emerging. . . .

The Earnshaw family has fallen into decay. The need is to rejuvenate it. The various characters, generally acting quite misguidedly for motives of their own, in fact are working steadily towards this end. Surrounding these actions is an aura of magic, of control from "beyond." Earnshaw has sought to help out a homeless waif. Hindley has acted to indulge his love. Catherine has acted to "raise" Heathcliff. All of these seem to have been serious mistakes, but in the grand design, they are all essential acts. Hindley, trying desperately to recoup his fortune, gambles away his patrimony to Heathcliff. Finally he even tries to kill Heathcliff, in order to do Hareton "justice," to prevent his being a "beggar." He fails. Here is the other side of the pattern working. The novel's characters are successful in every action which advances the design; they are abject failures in every under-taking counter to it. In this case, for example, suppose Hind-ley had not lost the house to Heathcliff, or suppose he had actually killed him. He would still have gambled or dissi-pated his money away, and the house would have gone to strangers, and Hareton would genuinely have been a beggar. It is Heathcliff's business acumen which ultimately pre-serves the property for Hareton. Hindley now, having per-formed his essential action, which was to lose the property to Heathcliff, falls, despite his iron constitution, into imme-diate decline and death.

Isabella lives long enough to raise Linton into adoles-cence . . . and dies. Edgar Linton lives long enough to raise Cathy in some civilization, and to bless her marriage with young Linton. Isabella's hopes that Heathcliff will not get the keeping of Linton and Edgar Linton's feckless last-minute attempts to keep Cathy financially independent of Heathcliff are both frustrated, but it is necessary for the grand design that they be.

HEATHCLIFF'S NATURAL POWER

We are down to Heathcliff, old Earnshaw's seemingly ill-advised adoption. Here, it seems to me, is the prime mover behind it all. As Dorothy Van Ghent suggests, Heathcliff, with his "gypsy lack of origins, his lack of orientation and determination in the social world, his equivocal status on the edge of the human . . . might *really* be a demon." Let us accept that he is. Surely his power is inordinate. Critics, peering through the novel's imagery, have seen him as a great natural force, as an immense sexual energy. Let us ex-amine the uses made of this power.

First, the three children, Cathy, Linton, Hareton, are all necessary to the successful resolution of the action. Thomas Moser, in an amusing and convincing Freudian interpreta-tion of the novel, has shown that Heathcliff, as a sort of irre-sistibly fertile incubus, may be implicated in the conceiving of all three of these. Obviously he impregnated Isabella, and on the first night, since it is inconceivable that they ever shared a bed again. Then, we remember, Catherine lived unproductively for six months with Edgar: "The gunpowder lay as harmless as sand, because no fire came near to ex-plode it." Then Heathcliff (often enough equated with fire and lightning) comes near, and precisely seven months later, Catherine bears "a puny, seven months' child." In view of this, we look suspiciously at the fact that it was nine months after Frances came to the house (where Heathcliff was) that she gave birth.

In other ways, sometimes more obviously, sometimes more remotely, Heathcliff's power can be seen operating on the plot. It was necessary for Catherine to marry Linton: she does it at least partly with the object of helping Heathcliff; Heathcliff it is who saves Hareton, walking under the stairs just as Hindley has dropped him; it is Heathcliff running off into exile which, properly to his demon character causes a tremendous lightning storm in which Catherine catches the chill she later transmits to the elder Lintons, effectively killing them off. It was necessary to have them out of the way so that the younger Lintons would be unprotected against the machinations of Catherine and Heathcliff.

Heathcliff's power seems to have an irresistible attractiveness to some of the characters which makes them ignore all well-intentioned advice about his remorselessness. Old Earnshaw is attracted to him, in the first place, thinking him "a gift of God," though the others see only a dirty, ragged "gipsy brat." Isabella is strongly enough attracted to elope with him, though Catherine has told her in no uncertain terms that he is "an unreclaimed creature . . . [a] wilderness of furze and whinstone . . . fierce, pitiless, wolfish." In this description is the secret of Catherine's own attraction to Heathcliff: he is a natural force; he has no soul, no ethical sense in the ordinary meaning; he is natural power, ruthless perhaps, but effective. "My love for Heathcliff resembles the eternal rocks beneath—a source of little visible delight, but necessary." And it has been necessary that each of these characters—Earnshaw, who adopts him, Catherine, who marries Linton for him, and Isabella, who gives him a son— it has been necessary to the Action of the novel that each of these be attracted to him. One more character must be: Cathy. But her attraction is displaced into the symbolism of the novel. "How long will it be," she asks Nelly, "before I can walk to the top of those hills?" She is speaking of Penistone Crags, steep cliffs rising out of the heath—a literal heath cliff. Nelly seeks to dissuade her, telling her "they were bare masses of stone ["the eternal rocks beneath"] with hardly enough earth in their clefts to nourish a stunted tree." "Papa would tell you, Miss . . . that they are not worth the trouble of climbing." But in the face of this advice, Cathy, just like the others, sets out after them, and on the way runs directly on to Heathcliff.

Much has been made of Heathcliff's revenge motive. It is there of course: superficially he is motivated by his hatred of the characters. But this is only his conscious motive, just as Earnshaw, consciously, was only doing a good turn, and Catherine, consciously, was marrying Edgar to raise Heathcliff. But at the same time that he shows and feels his hatred, much is made of the fact that he holds this hatred in check. When he is beating Hindley, for example, "he exerted preterhuman self-denial in abstaining from finishing him completely." He hasn't control of the house yet; his plan comes before every thought of revenge.

THE NEXT GENERATION

Critics have already belabored the fact that the novel's second half symmetrically duplicates the first half. I only want here to point out the particular way in which the second half matches the first, and to show how this matching was entirely Heathcliff's doing. Too much has been made of the fact that Heathcliff was merely getting even with Hindley and the Lintons. Let us ignore this, and see what his actions actually are. What he does is to reproduce a certain moment in the first half of the novel: that moment at which Catherine has married Edgar Linton, and Heathcliff has vanished. Hareton, as everyone knows, takes Heathcliff's place in the second generation. In the first generation, Hindley, the master of Wuthering Heights, for purposes of revenge thrusts Heathcliff out into the fields, to let him degenerate socially and intellectually, in order to separate him from Catherine. In the second generation, Heathcliff, the master of Wuthering Heights, for purposes of revenge thrusts Hareton out into the fields, to let him degenerate socially and intellectually, effectively separating him from Cathy. Hareton is the dispossessed rightful heir of the Heights, just as Heathcliff was, if (as I have suggested) he is the spiritual embodiment of old Earnshaw's first son, Heathcliff.

Linton obviously represents, in the new generation, Edgar Linton. Heathcliff, though supposedly also seeking revenge on him, does not barbarize him. He lets Isabella raise him until she dies, and after he takes him over, however much he hates him, still he takes good care of him (over and over again in all his machinations Heathcliff acts against his personal feelings, his design always taking precedence over his emotion of hatred). "In fact," Heathcliff says, "I've arranged everything with a view to preserve the superior and the gentleman in him." He will be just like Edgar, then, so that Cathy can be reasonably attracted to him (even though his weakness and selfishness stand out in greater relief than Edgar's) and eventually—though this took some forcing—marry him.

There is the original situation, then. Hareton-Heathcliff a barbarian banished to the fields. Cathy, spoiled and immature, marrying for all the wrong reasons—the weak and selfish, but genteel Linton. But now comes the change. This time, the situation is going to come out properly. Before, the healthy Catherine had died, and the sickly Edgar lived on; this time Linton dies quickly, while Cathy's health is unbroken. At Linton's death, Heathcliff cannot help exulting. "How do you feel, Catherine?" Twice he asks Cathy this (calling her by the name usually reserved for the first-generation Catherine). "He's safe, and I'm free." Perhaps this is exactly the answer he wants. Clearly there will be no lifelong mourning here, for her relationship with Linton was too trivial. Heathcliff has proved to his satisfaction, perhaps, that Catherine's marriage to Edgar Linton was no more than this.

In the succeeding passages of the novel, Heathcliff, for all his seeming hatred of Cathy, his seeming wish to be revenged on Hareton, actually does everything to thrust them together. Gratuitously, he takes all Cathy's books away from her, putting her more on Hareton's level, and also leaving her absolutely no diversion but his company. More and more Heathcliff leaves the house to them, shuns Hareton's company, and forces him to stay in the room where Cathy is sitting. Critics who do not like this part of the book feel that Cathy merely pretties up and domesticates Hareton, to his great loss. The interesting thing to me is how closely Hareton follows Heathcliff's own childhood actions. First he enlists Zillah's aid in getting himself made presentable, just as Heathcliff long before had let Nelly scrub him clean to be presentable for Catherine. If Heathcliff had wanted revenge, at this point he would have banished Hareton from Cathy's company, which is what Hindley had done to him in the similar situation. Precisely the same holds for the learning-to-read passages, for when Hindley first separated Heathcliff from the family, "Heathcliff bore his degradation pretty well at first, because Cathy taught him what she learnt." But Hindley makes it too hard for him. "He struggled long to keep up an equality with Catherine in her studies and yielded with poignant though silent regret: but he yielded completely." Properly, the revenge-seeking Heathcliff should have discouraged Cathy's attempts to educate Hareton. But he does not, for the underlying plan is to make things come out right, the way they should have the first time. Heathcliff seems as unconscious as the other characters of the success of his plan. It had seemed a mistake when Earnshaw took in Heathcliff, it had seemed a mistake when Catherine married Edgar, when Isabella married Heathcliff; it had seemed a failure when Hindley lost the Heights to Heathcliff, and Edgar lost the Grange. But as I have been pointing out, these superficial failures were all clear successes for the underlying plan. This is true again with Heathcliff. He seems to have failed at his revenge. "It is a poor conclusion, is it not," he observes to Nelly. "An absurd termination to my violent exertions." But the underlying design, of recreating the original situation (by this time he has even moved Nelly back into the household), so that it could come out properly this time, has been a success. He has played his essential role in it, and having done so, he, like the others, goes from robust health into immediate decline.

Theme and Method in Brontë's Seventh Chapter

William E. Buckler

Brontë approaches her novel with a "double vision of life and art" in chapter 7 of *Wuthering Heights*, explains University of Illinois English instructor William E. Buckler. It is in this chapter, he says, that she determines the direction of the rest of the novel after the triumphant return of Catherine—transformed from a rough tomboy into a cultivated young lady—to Wuthering Heights. Important characters are set in "proper relation" to each other, Heathcliff resolves to seek revenge on Hindley for the humiliation he has suffered, and Nelly Dean is established as a narrator the reader can trust. Had Brontë not written this crucial chapter with such deliberation, the events and themes of the remaining chapters would not be convincing.

From various critics we can obtain positive and judicious analyses of the general method of *Wuthering Heights* and of the advantages rising out of that method. But there is one crucial chapter, I think, in which we can see Emily Brontë conscientiously at work combining her theme and her method. In Chapter VII, the author looks forward with a double vision—of life and of art. And so many crucial elements are here amassed that it would surely be unthinkable that they were the result of anything less than careful and intentional planning.

THE CHARACTERS

Cathy returns from Thrushcross Grange quite the beautiful young lady. The five weeks that have so revolutionized her appearance, however, have had quite the opposite effect on

Excerpted from William E. Buckler, "Chapter VII of *Wuthering Heights*: A Key to Interpretation," *Nineteenth-Century Fiction*, vol. 7, no. 1, pp. 51–55. Copyright © 1952 by The Regents of the University of California. Used by permission of the University of California Press.

Heathcliff: careless and uncared for, he now looks a very "forbidding young blackguard" indeed. But there is something more to the scene than the contrast which gives Hindley and Frances such mean satisfaction. Cathy wants to have it both ways: she will love and embrace Heathcliff; but she would not have his dusky fingers mar her "grand plaid silk frock." And Cathy's selfishness prevents her from understanding how this desire on her part leads Heathcliff to revolt.

Heathcliff's isolation, however, is not yet complete. He goes to bed "dumb and dour"; but his struggle with himself in bed that night and on the moors the next morning must have been gigantic. The victorious result thereof brings Heathcliff to his highest point of courage and goodwill in the whole novel: "'Nelly, make me decent, I'm going to be good.'" In this state he realizes that power and revolt will not get him what he wants, Cathy's love. Nelly comforts, combs, and admonishes him concerning the evils of a proud heart; and with her enthusiastic conjectures concerning his high birth, she smooths away his frown and makes him pleasantly eager for the return of the family from church.

The scene then becomes crucial. All the characters of importance are brought together: Heathcliff, Cathy, Hindley, Edgar, and Isabella. Heathcliff, hastening to "show his amiable humour," has his guard completely down; and Hindley plunges his brutal dagger to the hilt. Thus at his most sensitive moment, after he has broken down his isolation in a tremendous inner struggle, Heathcliff is frustrated by Hindley in his attempt to express this fellow feeling by joining in the social festivities: he is abused, flogged, and locked in his chamber. Heathcliff's wrath, therefore, must center on Hindley, though Edgar—honest and determined, petted and weak—earns his portion more by accident than by intent. Isabella peevishly sets up a lament to go home. And Cathy, "confounded, blushing for all," expostulates with Edgar for having caused, unwittingly, Heathcliff's punishment. In the day of purgatory which followed, Cathy should have learned that she could not have it both ways. Even the quasi-happiness of her self-indulgence with the one would be destroyed by her passion for the other.

It is impossible to say what was the nature of the communion between Heathcliff and Cathy when she slipped away to join him in the garret that evening; but we do know that this day had changed Heathcliff from boyhood to manhood, had set the purpose of his life. This is made abundantly clear by the conversation between him and Nelly Dean in the kitchen that night:

> "I'm trying to settle how I shall pay Hindley back. I don't care how long I wait, if I can only do it at last. I hope he will not die before I do!"
>
> "For shame, Heathcliff!" said I. "It is for God to punish wicked people; we should learn to forgive."
>
> "No, God won't have the satisfaction that I shall," he returned. "I only wish I knew the best way! Let me alone, and I'll plan it out: while I'm thinking of that I don't feel pain."

Heathcliff's isolation is now complete: all pity gone, the "moral teething" has begun; and he will "grind with greater energy, in proportion to the increase of pain."

THE STORYTELLER

Then, with a noteworthy abruptness, Emily Brontë turns to the one other task which must be accomplished before the tragedy can move forward: the establishment of the character of her narrator. The first climax of the novel has been reached; the author's direction has been set. Nelly Dean, too, has already become commentator as well as storyteller: she has admonished Heathcliff about the evils of a proud heart; she has been watchful of Cathy's reaction to his punishment; and she has warned him against usurping the prerogative of God. She has shown that she will not only recount the action of the characters, but also pass value judgments on them; in short, she will be the author's authority in the novel. Henry James postulated that a novel needed one keen and trustworthy mind or intelligence, placed in the center of the main dramatic situation, to evaluate all its action. Since Nelly Dean was to be this central intelligence, Emily Brontë obviously thought that at this point she must put Nelly's qualifications before the reader. This she does with obvious care in the last twelve paragraphs of the chapter. Nelly Dean is a person of principles and convictions who could tell Heathcliff's history "in a half-a-dozen words." She has the qualities of thrift and energy which keep her in character as a Yorkshire housekeeper; but she has much more. She is thoughtful, reflective, "a steady, reasonable kind of body," with a wisdom taught by the "sharp discipline" of experience and by books. Nor does she look upon her story as something above or even outside of the main course of human experience. She is puzzled by the suggestion that her qualities of mind have come from "living among the hills and seeing one set of faces, and one series of actions, from year's end to year's end. . . ." Rather, she insists: "here we are the same as anywhere else, when you get to know us. . . ."

In Chapter VII, therefore, Emily Brontë sets significant signposts relative both to her theme and to her method: the important characters are put into proper relation one to the other; Heathcliff becomes determined in his "sin"; and the trustworthiness of the narrator is established.

Charlotte Brontë's Preface to *Wuthering Heights*

Charlotte Brontë

The preface to the second edition of *Wuthering Heights,* by Charlotte Brontë, Emily's elder sister and author of *Jane Eyre,* is both a defense of and an apology for the novel. She claims the book was written in a "wild workshop, with simple tools, out of homely material," but to those critics who view the novel as nothing more than a "horror of great darkness," she is quick to point out the redeeming qualities of Nelly Dean and Edgar Linton, who ironically have not always been looked on favorably by readers. Charlotte makes no apologies for Heathcliff, however, who stands "completely unredeemed," and notes that it is scarcely ever advisable to create such a character.

I have just read over "Wuthering Heights," and, for the first time, have obtained a clear glimpse of what are termed (and, perhaps, really are) its faults; have gained a definite notion of how it appears to other people—to strangers who knew nothing of the author; who are unacquainted with the locality where the scenes of the story are laid; to whom the inhabitants, the customs, the natural characteristics of the outlying hills and hamlets in the West Riding of Yorkshire are things alien and unfamiliar.

To all such "Wuthering Heights" must appear a rude and strange production. The wild moors of the north of England can for them have no interest; the language, the manners, the very dwellings and household customs of the scattered inhabitants of those districts, must be to such readers in a great measure unintelligible, and—where intelligible—repulsive. Men and women who, perhaps naturally very calm, and with feelings moderate in degree, and little

Reprinted from Charlotte Brontë's Editor's Preface to the 2nd edition of *Wuthering Heights,* by Emily Brontë. This version appeared in the 1943 Random House edition.

marked in kind, have been trained from their cradle to ob-serve the utmost evenness of manner and guardedness of language, will hardly know what to make of the rough, strong utterance, the harshly manifested passions, the un-bridled aversions, and headlong partialities of unlettered moorland hinds and rugged moorland squires, who have grown up untaught and unchecked, except by mentors as harsh as themselves. A large class of readers, likewise, will suffer greatly from the introduction into the pages of this work of words printed with all their letters, which it has be-come the custom to represent by the initial and final letter only—a blank line filling the interval. I may as well say at once that, for this circumstance, it is out of my power to apologise; deeming it, myself, a rational plan to write words at full length. The practice of hinting by single letters those expletives with which profane and violent persons are wont to garnish their discourse, strikes me as a proceeding which, however well meant, is weak and futile. I cannot tell what good it does—what feeling it spares—what horror it conceals.

With regard to the rusticity of "Wuthering Heights," I ad-mit the charge, for I feel the quality. It is rustic all through. It is moorish, and wild, and knotty as a root of heath. Nor was it natural that it should be otherwise; the author being her-self a native and nursling of the moors. Doubtless, had her lot been cast in a town, her writings, if she had written at all, would have possessed another character. Even had chance or taste led her to choose a similar subject, she would not have treated it otherwise. Had Ellis Bell been a lady or a gen-tleman accustomed to what is called "the world," her view of a remote and unreclaimed region, as well as of the dwellers therein, would have differed greatly from that actu-ally taken by the homebred country girl. Doubtless it would have been wider—more comprehensive: whether it would have been more original or more truthful is not so certain. As far as the scenery and locality are concerned, it could scarcely have been so sympathetic: Ellis Bell did not de-scribe as one whose eye and taste alone found pleasure in the prospect; her native hills were far more to her than a spectacle; they were what she lived in, and by, as much as the wild birds, their tenants, or as the heather, their produce. Her descriptions, then, of natural scenery, are what they should be, and all they should be.

EMILY'S LACK OF PRACTICAL KNOWLEDGE

Where delineation of human character is concerned, the case is different. I am bound to avow that she had scarcely more practical knowledge of the peasantry amongst whom she lived, than a nun has of the country people who sometimes pass her convent gates. My sister's disposition was not naturally gregarious; circumstances favoured and fostered her tendency to seclusion; except to go to church or take a walk on the hills, she rarely crossed the threshold of home. Though her feelings for the people round was benevolent, intercourse with them she never sought; nor, with very few exceptions, ever experienced. And yet she knew them: knew their ways, their language, their family histories; she could hear of them with interest, and talk of them with detail, minute, graphic, and accurate; but *with* them, she rarely exchanged a word. Hence it ensued that what her mind had gathered of the real concerning them was too exclusively confined to those tragic and terrible traits of which, in listening to the secret annals of every rude vicinage, the memory is sometimes compelled to receive the impress. Her imagination, which was a spirit more sombre than sunny, more powerful than sportive, found in such traits material whence it wrought creations like Heathcliff, like Earnshaw, like Catherine. Having formed these beings she did not know what she had done. If the auditor of her work when read in manuscript, shuddered under the grinding influence of natures so relentless and implacable, of spirits so lost and fallen; if it was complained that the mere hearing of certain vivid and fearful scenes banished sleep by night, and disturbed mental peace by day, Ellis Bell would wonder what was meant, and suspect the complainant of affectation. Had she but lived, her mind would of itself have grown like a strong tree, loftier, straighter, wider-spreading, and its matured fruits would have attained a mellower ripeness and sunnier bloom; but on that mind time and experience alone could work: to the influence of other intellects, it was not amenable.

NELLY AND EDGAR ARE SAVING GRACES

Having avowed that over much of "Wuthering Heights" there broods "a horror of great darkness"; that, in its storm-heated and electrical atmosphere, we seem at times to breathe lightning, let me point to those spots where clouded daylight and the eclipsed sun still attest their existence. For a specimen of true benevolence and homely fidelity, look at the character of Nelly Dean; for an example of constancy and tenderness, remark that of Edgar Linton. (Some people will think these qualities do not shine so well incarnate in a man as they would do in a woman, but Ellis Bell could never be brought to comprehend this notion: nothing moved her more than any insinuation that the faithfulness and clemency, the long-suffering and loving-kindness which are esteemed virtues in the daughters of Eve, become foibles in the sons of Adam. She held that mercy and forgiveness are the divinest attributes of the Great Being who made both man and woman, and that what clothes the Godhead in glory, can disgrace no form of feeble humanity.) There is a dry saturnine humour in the delineation of old Joseph, and some glimpses of grace and gaiety animate the younger Catherine. Nor is even the first heroine of the name destitute of a certain strange beauty in her fierceness, or of honesty in the midst of perverted passion and passionate perversity.

Heathcliff, indeed, stands unredeemed; never once swerving in his arrow-straight course to perdition, from the time when "the little black-haired swarthy thing, as dark as if it came from the Devil," was first unrolled out of the bundle and set on its feet in the farmhouse kitchen, to the hour when Nelly Dean found the grim, stalwart corpse laid on its back in the panel-enclosed bed, with wide-gazing eyes that seemed "to sneer at her attempt to close them, and parted lips and sharp white teeth that sneered too."

HEATHCLIFF IS A GHOUL

Heathcliff betrays one solitary human feeling, and that is *not* his love for Catherine; which is a sentiment fierce and inhuman; a passion such as might boil and glow in the bad essence of some evil genius; a fire that might form the tormented centre—the ever-suffering soul of a magnate of the infernal world: and by its quenchless and ceaseless ravage effect the execution of the decree which dooms him to carry Hell with him wherever he wanders. No; the single link that connects Heathcliff with humanity is his rudely-confessed regard for Hareton Earnshaw—the young man whom he has ruined; and then his half-implied esteem for Nelly Dean. These solitary traits omitted, we should say he was child

LESBIANISM AND THE CENSORING OF *WUTHERING HEIGHTS*
Jean E. Kennard claims that Charlotte Brontë, through the editing and possible destruction of some of Emily's writing, attempted to censor her life and her work. While she does not claim that Emily was a lesbian by today's definition of the words, she says Charlotte hoped to hide information about Emily's ambiguous sexual identity that might bring shame on the family.

As editor of the 1850 edition of her sister's novel *Wuthering Heights*, Charlotte Brontë attempted what political discourse now calls "a spin." In her preface she apologized for Heathcliff, proposed Edgar Linton and Nelly Dean as compensating models of virtue, and adopted the role of mediator between Emily Brontë and an uncomprehending Victorian public, many of whom had seen the novel as unnatural and its author as disturbed. In addition, Charlotte's editing, which diluted Emily's diction and regulated the rhythms of her syntax by altering the punctuation, amounted "virtually to a writing down of the novel," U.C. Knoepflmacher says. It also seems probable that Charlotte destroyed her sister's posthumous papers. She published only 17 of the 103 poems extant after Emily's death, and those she reworked. There are no remaining letters between Emily and her family, no prose juvenilia, and very few diary entries, although we know that Emily wrote frequently to her sister Anne when they were apart and kept a diary. Charlotte herself acknowledged that manuscripts of her sister's writings existed after her death. . . .

I suggest that Charlotte's censorship of Emily's life and work is far more typical of someone who is trying to hide information she thinks of as shameful, information that, if revealed, would damage not only her sister's reputation but by association her own and that of her family. This essay suggests an alternative hypothesis: that it was Emily Brontë's lesbianism that Charlotte knew of, feared the revelation of in *Wuthering Heights*, and was attempting to suppress.

I do not claim that Emily Brontë was a lesbian in any modern sense of the term. . . . Nor am I claiming that Emily consciously set out to encode homosexuality in *Wuthering Heights*. I am suggesting that her ambivalence about what she perceived as her sexual identity reveals itself in a variety of ways in the novel. . . . *Wuthering Heights* both reveals and controls Emily's sexual identity. It contains a form of self-censorship that licenses not only her sister but subsequent critics to suppress what Emily found unacceptable in herself.

Jean E. Kennard, "Lesbianism and the Censoring of *Wuthering Heights*," *NWSA Journal*, vol. 8, no. 2, Summer 1996, pp. 17–36.

neither of Lascar nor gipsy, but a man's shape animated by demon life—a Ghoul—an Afreet.

Whether it is right or advisable to create beings like Heathcliff, I do not know: I scarcely think it is. But this I know: the writer who possesses the creative gift owns something of which he is not always master—something that, at times, strangely wills and works for itself. He may lay down rules and devise principles, and to rules and principles it will perhaps for years lie in subjection; and then, haply without any warning of revolt, there comes a time when it will no longer consent to "harrow the valleys, or be bound with a band in the furrow"—when it "laughs at the multitude of the city, and regards not the crying of the driver"—when, refusing absolutely to make ropes out of sea-sand any longer, it sets to work on statue-hewing, and you have a Pluto or a Jove, a Tisiphone or a Psyche, a Mermaid or a Madonna, as Fate or Inspiration direct. Be the work grim or glorious, dread or divine, you have little choice left but quiescent adoption. As for you—the nominal artist—your share in it has been to work passively under dictates you neither delivered nor could question—that would not be uttered at your prayer, nor suppressed nor changed at your caprice. If the result be attractive, the World will praise you, who little deserve praise; if it be repulsive, the same World will blame you, who almost as little deserve blame.

"Wuthering Heights" was hewn in a wild workshop, with simple tools, out of homely materials. The statuary found a granite block on a solitary moor; gazing thereon, he saw how from the crag might be elicited a head, savage, swart, sinister; a form moulded with at least one element of grandeur—power. He wrought with a rude chisel, and from no model but the vision of his meditations. With time and labour, the crag took human shape; and there it stands colossal, dark, and frowning, half statue, half rock: in the former sense, terrible and goblinlike; in the latter, almost beautiful, for its colouring is of mellow grey, and moorland moss clothes it; and heath, with its blooming bells and balmy fragrance, grows faithfully close to the giant's foot.

The Epic Heritage of *Wuthering Heights*

Vereen Bell

Assistant professor of English at Vanderbilt University Vereen Bell argues that *Wuthering Heights* draws heavily on traditions of storytelling that predate the Victorian formulas of Brontë's day. Brontë's work, he says, embraces folktales and legends of the British Isles and the tradition of oral narrative popular within her own family. Like the best epic poems, Bell explains, Brontë's novel makes powerful use of its storytelling narrator and character monologues. While Brontë's characters remain flat, or undeveloped, Bell says that, as in the world of the ballad, they should not be held up to the "confines of historical definition"; they are successful in that they are psychologically real.

Within its historical context *Wuthering Heights* is remarkable not so much because of its emotional excess as because of the austerity of its design. Without the densely configured social world of earlier English fiction, its realm seems almost oppressively cosmic; its power and intensity are achieved with a sacrifice of human vitality. Yet of course Emily Brontë ignored the conventional human landscape—of inn-keepers and lawyers and thieves—because this was a world which she knew largely nothing about. Her protagonists, whatever they may be symbolically, as social beings are without models and prototypes in our experience. Moreover, because she was intellectually as well as socially isolated, her novel as a whole, like her characters, is distinctly atypical. [Lord David Cecil writes:] "Since she had no ready-made conventions to help her, since she always had to invent them for herself, her form is appropriate to her conception, as it could never have been if she had tried to mold her inspiration to fit the accepted Vic-

Excerpted from Vereen Bell, "*Wuthering Heights* as Epos," *College English*, vol. 25, no. 3 (December 1963), pp. 199–208. Reprinted courtesy of the National Council of Teachers of English.

torian formulas." Her most remarkable achievement was in turning her limitations to advantage.

On the other hand *Wuthering Heights* is unique mainly as a hybrid. However little it may have in common with other Victorian fiction, it draws heavily upon older conventions of story, conventions known to Emily Brontë in the fugitive and unprinted folk tales and legends of the British Isles. Within the Brontë family there was a tradition of oral narrative that we are not surprised to find affecting Emily's fiction. Patrick Brontë, we are told, frequently amused his children with lurid tales handed down through his father, Hugh Brunty, an Irish peasant who in his own day had been renowned as a storyteller; and Tabitha Ackroyd, the elderly servant, likewise engaged the children's fancy with tales of fairies and family tragedies. It is not unlikely that a sheltered girl, least tutored of the Brontës might have found in this familiar genre a natural, easy medium for rendering her conception.

Historically, of course, fiction, as we know it, owes its origins to the [epic] genre—specifically the mode "in which the radical of presentation is the author or minstrel as oral reciter, with a listening audience in front of him"; and in *Wuthering Heights*, a synthesis of spoken narrative conventions with those of the printed page, the novel form is clearly identified with this heritage. In choosing Nelly Dean as her point of view and oral narrative as her medium, Emily Brontë was able to give full expression to her limited creative gift.

NELLY AS STORYTELLER

The dominant structural mode of *Wuthering Heights* is oral— Nelly tells and Lockwood listens—and the narrative's technique is modified and controlled by this peculiar discipline. The nearest familiar analogue is perhaps the English folk ballad. Because of its rigid design the ballad, unlike the novel, must achieve unity of a special kind: "it must forego the novelist's privilege of description and explanation; it must forego . . . the leisure, the comfortable elaboration of the Epic." Nelly's technique is subject to the same conditions; her story is meant to be heard, not read; it must hit hard once and for all. The few symbolic effects of her narrative are sharp and uncomplicated, as they must be, since there is only one chance to convey the desired impression. Over-elaboration lulls the listener and the reader out of awareness.

Without Lockwood there to hear, Nelly would be address-
ing herself directly to the reader, and were that so, she
would be no longer speaking but writing. As a consequence
the whole complexion of her narrative would be altered; she
would incur new responsibilities for detail indigenous to the
novel. As it is, Nelly's sole responsibility is to the central action of her story; anything extraneous is cut away. It is often
remarked, for example, that the reader is always conscious
of the setting of *Wuthering Heights,* and yet the novel is all
but devoid of physical description. The few vivid impres-
sions we do have come from Lockwood. As the recorder he
is aware of his responsibility for placing us securely within
the natural and domestic environment of the action. From
his pen we learn of the exposed, wind-blown station of
Wuthering Heights; of the "stunted firs at the end of the
house," and the "range of gaunt thorns all stretching their
limbs one way, as if craving alms of the sun." Inside the
house his detail is meticulous.

> One end, indeed, reflected splendidly both light and heat
> from ranks of immense pewter dishes, interspersed with sil-
> ver jugs and tankards, towering row after row, in a vast oak
> dresser, to the very roof. The latter had never been under-
> drawn: its entire anatomy lay bare to an inquiring eye, except
> where a frame of wood laden with oatcakes, and clusters of
> legs of beef, mutton, and ham, concealed it. Above the chim-
> ney were sundry villainous old guns, and a couple of horse-
> pistols.

And so on. The style is frankly literary—that is, composed.
In Nelly's simple narrative such elaboration would be im-
plausible and inappropriate; she is confined to strictly relevant external detail. Frequently, for example, she refers to
the elements, but these allusions are always either pertinent
to the action—as when Catherine is stricken from soaking
herself in the rain—or evoked superstitiously in reverie as
rather primitive, symbolic preparation for events of great
moment. . . .
The more extensive and complicated evocations are left to
Lockwood. Because of this division of responsibility, and because Nelly's narrative comprises the major portion of the
book, explicit descriptive setting is naturally and plausibly
scarce. Were Nelly alone in her recollections—composing
instead of speaking—these peripheral descriptions as well
as the central action would fall within her province.

WUTHERING HEIGHTS **I**S A **S**TORY-**C**ENTERED **N**OVEL

Moreover, without embroidery, without extra detail, the entire concept of characterization is sharply modified. We can
see this discipline at work in the number of characters who
figure in Nelly's narrative. Supernumeraries are all but totally absent. Only wholly functional characters appear; all
others are severely pared away.

Nelly is responsible directly only to Lockwood, and her
range is consequently self-limited. Those figures who we
must assume impinged upon the life at Wuthering Heights
and the Grange—citizens of nearby Gimmerton, perhaps—
she almost wholly ignores. They are not her concern. She
has no need for humanizing touches. The linear, relentless
progress of events attenuates the shape of her narrative.
Unity understood in this narrow sense is rarely encountered
in the English novel, and the result in *Wuthering Heights* is
a seeming thinness of scope—for all its concentrated impact.

This same discipline has a similar devitalizing effect
upon individual character; but the loss in intimacy is more
than offset by a corresponding gain in emotional energy and
heightened symbolic emphasis. Catherine and Heathcliff are
vitalized by the intensity of Emily Brontë's imagination; but
as Lord David Cecil has phrased it, they are "more vivid than
real." Or in Northrop Frye's language, they are less "real
people" than "stylized figures which expand into psychological archetypes"—intensely emotional, perhaps, but stylized
just the same. Considering Emily Brontë's limited experience with people and the world, it is not surprising that her
central characters are not "real" in any conventional,
mimetic sense; but beyond that, the simplicity of the narrative medium, and of its agent Nelly Dean, imposes a kind of
aesthetic logic of its own.

Detail is so sparse in Nelly's account that we know next to
nothing about the routine of Catherine's and Heathcliff's
daily lives. So much is left to the reader's imagination in that
quarter that it fails to function at all. Of what Catherine does
when she is not tormenting a hapless admirer or lamenting
the bitter hostility between Edgar and Heathcliff; of what
Heathcliff does with himself when not cursing Catherine or
ruining Hindley and the children of three families, we can
have no idea. Incident unassociated with the grand torment
of Catherine and Heathcliff is discarded as superfluous. It is

characteristic of this method that Heathcliff can disappear for years and return to the Heights a wealthy and educated man without the slightest intelligence as to how this transformation was accomplished. Moreover, the limited point of view has again worked to advantage: were we to see Heathcliff, even briefly, in the process of making his fortune, he would necessarily be set into some kind of social and material context; and this definition would almost surely rob him of the essential demonic and archetypal qualities in his character. And of course no one cares where Heathcliff has been or what he has done, just as no reader really cares what happens to the figures when they are off-stage; the story itself is too absorbing, the emotional pitch too high for distractions to be desirable. But this very tautness points up the fact that *Wuthering Heights* is, after all, like the ballad, not character-centered but story-centered; the action determines how much we are to see of a given individual.

BRONTË'S CHARACTERS ARE PSYCHOLOGICALLY REAL

In a sense Emily Brontë's figures are flat characters, to use Forster's term, but this is not to say that they do not develop. With Catherine, for example, all but the most essential elements of character are refined away. Yet she is by no means static: time wears patiently at her wayward disposition, and when she dies, a haggard, beaten, and bewildered woman, she is far removed from the impetuous but compassionate spirit we knew as a girl. Heathcliff and Catherine, young Cathy and Hareton are all highly refined conceptions, and when time passes over them it is not to open new possibilities of personality, but to shape and maim those few given us at the start—only those in fact that are essential to the story. Because the story is made to be heard it must be delivered in the simplest and most vivid accents.

The struggle of Heathcliff and Catherine to merge their identities Nelly develops (in the ballad tradition) through a series of linked scenes. She is not above summarizing a period of three years or twelve, but these summary passages are brief, often barely a sentence, and the scenes are long. They are also revealing. There can be, of course, none of Dickens' elaboration of recurrent gesture, the leitmotifs that assist us in immediate recognition; nor is Nelly attentive to the efficacy or personal idiom, except with Joseph, whom even Isabella mocks as a sort of standing joke and who is very little else than an idiomatic Yorkshire chorus. As a consequence, though we may see the characters directly for the most part, we have some difficulty in conceiving for them a distinct social image.

Psychologically, however, they are fully known. Nelly has not the intellectual equipment for analysis, but her faithful (if improbable) rendering of dialogue does the job for her. She has no access to self-communings, but the scenes are selected with such care that private doubts and frustrations are repeatedly and emphatically suggested in dramatic action. So while we perceive only the essential aspect of character, that vital spirit is revolved about and centered upon until the inner conflict is forcefully dramatized. Typical of these revealing incidents is the significant scene that discloses young Heathcliff's apprehension when it appears that the bond between him and Catherine is about to be severed. Catherine is expecting her young friends from across the moor; when Heathcliff inquires pointedly about her silk frock she is at first evasive but finally finds it needful "to smooth the way for an intrusion."

> "Isabella and Edgar Linton talked of calling this afternoon. . . . As it rains, I hardly expect them; but, they may come, and if they do, you run the risk of being scolded for no good."
> "Order Ellen to say you are engaged, Cathy," he persisted. "Don't turn me out for those pitiful, silly friends of yours! I'm on the point, sometimes, of complaining that they—but I'll not—"
> "That they what?" cried Catherine, gazing at him with a troubled countenance. "Oh, Nelly!" she added petulantly, jerking her head away from my hands, "You've combed my hair quite out of curl! That's enough, let me alone. What are you on the point of complaining about, Heathcliff?"
> "Nothing—only look at the almanack, on that wall." He pointed to a framed sheet hanging near the window, and continued:
> "The crosses are for the evenings you have spent with the Lintons, the dots for those spent with me. Do you see? I've marked every day."
> "Yes—very foolish; as if I took notice!" replied Catherine in a peevish tone. "And where is the sense of that?"
> "To show you that I *do* take notice," said Heathcliff.
> "And should I always be sitting with you?" she demanded. . . . "What good do I get—what do you talk about? You might be dumb or a baby for anything you say to amuse me, or for anything you do, either!"
> "You never told me before that I talked too little, or that you

disliked my company, Cathy!" exclaimed Heathcliff in much agitation.

"It's no company at all, when people know nothing and say nothing," she muttered.

Here the scene is broken off by the entrance of Edgar Linton. Nothing is resolved; the painful tension is left unrelieved. But when this scene is merged easily with another in the next instant, the full effect upon Catherine becomes apparent. Unable to suppress her guilt, she explodes violently when Nelly seems impertinent, turns savagely upon little Hareton, and even strikes Linton when he tries to interfere. When she finally relieves her stress in tears, the reader is released momentarily to reflect and know the full meaning of Catherine's conflict between boundless love and the obstruction to its fulfillment in her and Heathcliff's disparate temperaments.

THE POWER OF MONOLOGUE

Dialogue, however, only suggests what is beneath the surface; to penetrate deeper, to explore the more subtle psychological and emotional states that are only intimated in dramatic action, Emily Brontë resorts to an adroit use of monologue, and, again to Nelly's faithful reporting. We are permitted to view another dimension of Catherine's character in several scenes in which Catherine almost unconsciously purges herself in a kind of compulsive articulation. Of such are Catherine's words in the aftermath of the reunion with Heathcliff and the terrible foredooming encounter with her unsympathetic husband. Distractedly she examines the feathers of her pillow torn with her teeth in a fit of frenzy.

> "That's a turkey's," she murmured to herself; "and this is a wild duck's; and this is a pigeon's. Ah, they put pigeons' feathers in the pillows—no wonder I couldn't die! Let me take care to throw it on the floor when I lie down. And here's a moorcock's; and this—I should know it among a thousand—it's a lapwing's. Bonny bird; wheeling over our heads in the middle of the moor. It wanted to get to its nest, for the clouds touched the swells, and it felt rain coming. This feather was picked up from the heath, the bird was not shot—we saw its nest in the winter, full of little skeletons. Heathcliff set a trap over it, and the old ones dare not come. I made him promise he'd never shoot a lapwing, after that, and he didn't. Yes, there are more! Did he shoot my lapwings, Nelly? Are they red, any of them?"

Symbolically in these words Catherine describes the tragedy of her existence—the tension between her will to freedom and her need of security, and finally Heathcliff's determined refusal to permit her to come to rest. Many years later the bird image recurs to disclose, ironically, precisely the opposite yearning of young Cathy's flickering spirit. A sullen, beaten prisoner in the dark household of Heathcliff, she sits alone, carving out of turnip parings "figures of birds and beasts." When Lockwood enlivens her somewhat with news of Nelly and home, she gazes distantly at the hills and murmurs with simple eloquence, "I should like to be riding Minny down there! I should like to be climbing up there— Oh! I'm tired—I'm *stalled*, Hareton!"

ECHOING THE EPIC

As a narrator Nelly makes the best of her limited opportunities. She does not embroider; her development is linear and pure; but it is always emphatically and sharply centered. The subtle currents of emotional energy are so tautly sustained that our disbelief is suspended, and Heathcliff's and Catherine's anguished love, intense beyond the sphere of social reality, is made both convincing and moving. Ultimately the inadvertent discipline of [the epic] works to advantage. Nelly cannot give us enough detail, Dickens-data, of telling gesture and idiom to individualize her people very sharply. They have not the hard edges of a social image. What is accomplished, however, is a fine balance between social and symbolic character. The inherent restrictions of her medium give us characters who are not so distinct, not so particularized as individuals that they cannot be easily extended outward into mythic figures; and yet they are not so highly abstracted that we cannot feel their pain and understand in them new depths of human suffering. The two concepts of characterization enforce each other; the human quality enforces the symbolic by adding the cogency of identification; the symbolic enforces the human by extending one strange event of history into the more enduring realm of myth. Both results are accomplished through an artful modification of traditional techniques of oral narrative. . . .

Like the ballad, Nelly's tale is not concerned with society at large but with an imprecise, fugitive world of its own and this concentration has the effect of releasing her characters from the confines of historical definition.

Again like the ballad, as the figures are independent of time they are also immune to ethical judgment. Nelly, it is true, utters opinions, but she is a character of the action, independent of the author's views and obviously not to be taken as a persona; her morality is patently superficial and therefore inadequate. Nelly's judgment is there in fact only to show how facile and incompetent human judgment can be. The love of Heathcliff and Catherine transcends all human standards of behavior; and by presenting their tragedy through one who has her own view Emily Brontë avoids taking on the responsibility for attempting the impossible, that is, passing an ultimate God-like judgment herself. Unappraised by a superior human intellect, Heathcliff and Catherine are left to move outside the moral realm. Nelly cannot pull them down to her level; her imagination does not soar. But she gives them life, and once they breathe they generate their own strength to transcend not only human values but the confines of life itself.

The Theme of Haunting

Rachel Trickett

Rachel Trickett, principal of St. Hugh's College in Oxford, England, concedes that *Wuthering Heights* ultimately is a love story, but asserts that Brontë first set out to write the "story of a haunting." Aspects of haunting are found in Heathcliff's obsessions and drive for possession of all that surrounds him, in Brontë's use of both the supernatural and natural worlds, and in the story's "defeat of a curse and reconciliation both of the spiritual and of the human pair." It is a story, Trickett says, told by observers who are "half in, half out of the ghost world but wholly of the physical one."

In *Wuthering Heights*, first of all, Emily Brontë set out to write the story of a haunting.

The book begins as the adventure of an introspective, romantic dandy, Lockwood, who fancies himself at odds with society after an abortive love-episode, and has buried himself in an improbable retreat in the Yorkshire moors. Snowbound on a visit to his landlord, he is the victim of an apparition which he can hardly distinguish as nightmare or fact. As he escapes from the room where this has happened, he observes his host, the grim eccentric farmer of his brief acquaintance, wildly invoking the spirit of the child who has disturbed his own rest or dreams, calling out from the open window through the storm in language which is of a quite different emotional quality from the Gothic horror of Lockwood's own experience: "Come in! Come in! Cathy, do come! Oh do—*once* more. Oh! my heart's darling, hear me *this* time, Catherine, at last".

After this, Lockwood returns to the milder house he has rented, Thrushcross Grange, and persuades his house-

Excerpted from Rachel Trickett, "*Wuthering Heights*: The Story of a Haunting," Brontë Society *Transactions*, vol. 16, no. 5 (1975), pp. 338–47. Reprinted by permission of the publisher.

keeper to identify the relationships of the people at the Heights. He falls ill as a result of his experience on that snowy night, and she enlivens his convalescence by relating to him the family history of the Lintons and the Earnshaws. . . . In Chapter XXXI we return to Lockwood who by now, like the reader, has become so completely drawn into the retrospective world of her story that he regains his position as narrator simply through his office as go-between from the Grange to the Heights, from Nelly Dean to young Catherine Linton. But the chapter concludes with a definite if slight wrench on the reader's attention as Lockwood prepares to return south with a reflection which restores him to his earlier dandyism:

> "How dreary life gets over in that house!" I reflected while riding down the road. "What a realisation of something more romantic than a fairy tale it would have been for Mrs. Linton Heathcliff had she and I struck up an attachment, as her good nurse desired, and migrated together into the stirring atmosphere of the town."

Lockwood is deluded about what the good nurse desires, but his parting observation succeeds momentarily in pushing the story back to its introduction where it was his adventure, his horror-tale, the events of a bad night and a narrative heard in illness around which all the feverishness of delirium still hangs. He does not return to Thrushcross Grange but, the following year, finding himself in the vicinity, he decides to visit the house and discover how the story has resolved itself. The whole scene and atmosphere have completely changed. Finding the Grange deserted, he goes to the Heights and witnesses an idyllic scene, rather like a Victorian genre painting, young Catherine teaching Hareton Earnshaw to read by the hearth. . . . Lockwood has already noticed the scent of wallflowers in the yard, and the picture of the open windows bringing air and freedom to the room is only the setting to the tutorial love-passage between Catherine and Hareton, "her shining ringlets blending at intervals with his brown locks". Then he becomes aware of Nelly Dean in her original place singing by the fire to the familiar accompaniment of Joseph's grumbling curses. It is a transformation scene, accounted for when Nelly tells Lockwood that his old landlord Heathcliff is dead. A spell has been broken. Nelly takes up her tale again simply to recount the slow decline of Heathcliff.

OBSESSION AND POSSESSION

Every stage of her story is part of a sequence of possession. Heathcliff, not Lockwood is the truly haunted man of the novel, and his haunting is like his obsession. He is possessed. He loses appetite for food or for life and even his rage cannot operate. When he recognises the growing affinity between Catherine and Hareton he can do nothing to prevent it. . . .

Later Heathcliff describes to Nelly the strange lethargy that possesses him—his inability to execute his revenge. "I have lost the faculty of enjoying their destruction". He explains his horror of Catherine's likeness to her mother. . . . When Nelly asks him if he anticipates or fears death, he replies:

> I cannot continue in this condition. I have to remind myself to breathe—almost to remind my heart to beat! And it is like bending back a stiff spring—it is by compulsion that I do the slightest act not prompted by one thought; and by compulsion that I notice anything, alive or dead which is not associated with the one universal idea. I have a single wish and my whole being and faculties are yearning to attain it. They have yearned towards it so long and so unwaveringly, that I'm convinced it will be reached—and soon, because it has devoured my existence: I am swallowed up in the anticipation of its fulfilment.

These are the terms of obsession and dedication as well as of haunting. Sometimes the words Heathcliff uses are yet more extreme: "it has devoured my existence". The stages of his self-immolation are traced by Nelly in terms of Gothic horror. She sees Heathcliff as a goblin, a ghoul or a vampire. The night before his death, like Lockwood in the opening chapter, she dreams a dream, but hers is of the whole existence of Heathcliff since he first appeared at the Heights: "where did he come from, the little dark thing, harboured by a good man to his bane?" She says that superstition prompted the dream of Heathcliff's death and funeral, and of the carving of his single name on his tomb. But superstition is a natural response to his singularity, and he speaks of his own condition in language both strange and extreme: "My soul's bliss kills my body but does not satisfy itself". In answer to Nelly's reminder of his unchristian life, her suggestion that he should repent or see a minister, he lapses into the language of melodrama to try to force her to understand his curious state of ecstasy: "By God! she's relentless. Oh!

damn it! It's *unutterably* too much for flesh and blood to bear, even mine". And in this crude exclamation there is an echo of an earlier lingering death—Cathy's, and her assertion, "I shall be *incomparably* beyond and above you all".

The haunting which is a matter of horror and superstition to the onlookers has however for Heathcliff some benign effects. It is expiatory; it removes from him the power to carry out his planned revenge. It is the necessary prelude to his death and reunion with Cathy. The discovery of Heathcliff's body in the same room in which Lockwood's first experience took place, recalls in each small detail that opening. "The lattice flapping to and fro", the open window, the grazed hand, this time Heathcliff's not the ghostly Cathy's, and there is now no blood trickling from the broken skin, from which Nelly infers that he is 'dead and stark'. Joseph's elegy is in keeping with the superstitious horror Heathcliff excites in the servants: "The divil's harried off his soul, and he must hev his carcass into 't bargain for owt I care!" Of Catherine's reaction we hear nothing, but we see Hareton's passionate grief though Heathcliff had tried to repeat in him a parody of his own original degradation by Hareton's father Hindley, as a revenge for it. The revenge he has been restrained from fulfilling rebounds on him; where Heathcliff meant to sow hatred, he has raised love. Nelly tells Lockwood that the country people say he walks. Joseph sitting in the Heights at the window claims to have seen 'the two of them' every night since Heathcliff's death. A crying child confesses he has been frightened on the moors: "There's Heathcliff and a woman yonder, under 't nab un I darunt pass 'em". Nelly herself does not like to walk out alone on the moors or stay alone at the Heights. . . .

At this stage few readers fail to recall the opening picture of that kitchen, dark and fire-lit, heaving with the mass of the bitch and her puppies, the sullen girl, the brutish boy and the demonic farmer of the first chapter. The spell has indeed been broken. Joseph, as in a fairy tale, is left in the haunted house while the two lovers and the homely nurse return to their proper place in an unenchanted world. Ordinary life takes over again. The celebrated last paragraph of the novel is not Nelly's, however, it is Lockwood's, and in it he is scouting superstition. He wonders how anyone could ever imagine unquiet slumbers for the sleepers in that quiet earth. It is a rational conclusion, but Nelly as well as Joseph and the crying child can imagine it; the end of the novel is an unanswered question. . . .

THE NATURAL AND SUPERNATURAL

Let us consider that art more closely. It has often been observed that all the trappings of the Gothic novel are there in *Wuthering Heights*. But as Nelly's narrative, at once commonplace and fearful in her attitude to its events, holds our sense of the supernatural in check, so Lockwood's first experience which begins the haunting is matched by his final comment which takes us back to the world of benignant nature. We are never allowed to come down finally on one side or the other. As in all good ghost stories a haunting is only possible if there is a palpable material world and living human beings to be haunted. Emily Brontë's great skill is her placing of these human beings, the way in which she ranges them round the two central characters Cathy and Heathcliff in varying degrees of consciousness of their absolute world. The servants, Joseph, Zillah and Nelly are at one remove; Lockwood is even further. The narrative is carried on by the outsider Lockwood first and last, but the main part of the story is told by Nelly the insider. Yet she, too, is separated from Cathy and Heathcliff, though so close to them, by her inability to apprehend their mode of experience. Between the two extremes of these narrators and Heathcliff and Cathy lie the younger generation—Catherine and Hareton, siblings, physically connected with the elder pair, sharing something of the same nature, who occupy a secondary yet quasi-central position in the book. That position itself reveals Emily Brontë's intention in her story.

She had not decided to write a tragedy, though *Wuthering Heights* is often spoken of as tragic because of its intensity and power. She was working out instead a story of reconciliation, of the sins and errors of the parents redeemed by the loves of the children. Heathcliff's son Linton is sacrificed early to make way for his surrogate, Cathy's nephew Hareton whom Heathcliff means to degrade as his father Hindley had degraded him. But Hareton shares some of his aunt Cathy's nature and Heathcliff recognises it; his inarticulate love for Heathcliff is an important element in the reconciliation theme—expiating his father's contempt and arrogance. Both Hareton and Catherine are nearer to the absolute vision of Heathcliff and Cathy than they are to Nelly's world.

Yet it is significant that Nelly loves the younger Catherine as she had never loved her mother; in the daughter there is a closer approximation to the natural and ordinary world. Though Lockwood at first sees the young pair as appropriate inhabitants of Wuthering Heights—a beautiful witch and a young boor, Nelly's story prepares us for a better understanding of their mediate position. They inhabit a half-and-half world which we should hardly have expected Emily Brontë to have recognised, cared about or understood. . . .

The realism of *Wuthering Heights* may be more apparent to Northerners even at this time, than to others. Emily Brontë did not have to invent Joseph or Nelly Dean. The cussed fanaticism of the one, the self-preserving mixture of unshockability and censoriousness of the other exist to this day as locally recognisable. But she had to realise the way in which these types could be used to further her ends. Nelly's and Joseph's world is a savage one, and Emily Brontë depicts it with the same matter of fact acceptance as her main narrator. What shocks and disturbs Lockwood—savage dogs, physical violence, verbal outrage—the other characters accept without comment. Equally Nelly can describe her fear of Heathcliff and her exasperation with Cathy to Lockwood, but she entertains and accepts them in her world in a way that he can't.

The violence of *Wuthering Heights* is extraordinary even for a Gothic tale in its harsh ferocity. It seems to be epitomised in the recurrent incidents of mauling dogs—from the first experience of Lockwood to the creatures that savage Heathcliff and Cathy when they peer through the windows of Thrushcross Grange. Or in Heathcliff's gratuitous act of sadism when he hangs Isabella's puppy. These are characteristic of the prevalent idea of torment, physical, mental and spiritual, an idea that Emily Brontë entertains familiarly and unflinchingly. It is worth asking why, given all this, the novel could never be cited as obscene or sadistic. Its ingredients might seem to be those of any modern Gothic sensation story—a mixture of passionate perverse love, violence and hatred, and yet it is a work of such singular purity that no one has ever suggested banning it or been afraid of a child reading it. The reason is two-fold: first the complete and unquestioning conviction with which Emily Brontë presents her extraordinary hero and heroine and their view of experience, and second her recognition that to everyone else in the book this view, to her so familiar, is in some degree antipathetic, strange or horrifying. To be able to entertain these two conflicting attitudes and reconcile them in a work of fiction is an achievement of genuine artistry as well as of natural genius. . . .

Cathy is condemned as wild and cruel and self-indulgent by Nelly, but she never for a moment loses her position as heroine. Heathcliff is even more a force of destruction though Lockwood sees some distinction in his barbarity and Nelly some cause for his savagery. But he remains the pivotal figure of the book, solitary and unconnected (it is important that his son, the fruit of his parody marriage to Isabella should die), except through his ultimate affinity with Cathy. He remains a figure uncontaminated by human relationships in the normal sense of the term. He and Cathy have the power of the absolute, of the natural and supernatural combined to such a degree that the dimension in which they exist can only be communicated to the other figures in the novel as ghostly. A story of complex experience, from the simple and brutal to the visionary, is brilliantly told to us as the story of a haunting. Emily Brontë's view of reality is at once so subtle and so pure that, outside lyric poetry, she saw the best mode of expressing it as that of the ghost tale.

BRONTË'S DOUBLE VISION

But she was not content with the single vision. The isolation of Cathy and Heathcliff is modified by the reconciliation of the younger pair; the vision of spiritual affinity is interwoven with the picture of ordinary human suffering and ordinary human happiness. With a kind of ironic tolerance, Emily Brontë displays the gulf between common existence and the essential principle of vitality that lies behind it, and bridges it with astonishing skill. . . .

So the story of a haunting involves the defeat of a curse and the reconciliation both of the spiritual and of the human pair. It turns out to be a love story, not a horror story, and one that involves every range of love from the essential to the simple and natural, from the loyal and affectionate to the trivial and fanciful in Lockwood's silly day dreams. . . .

[*Wuthering Heights*] defeats our provisional interpretations and reveals its meaning on its own terms—best, perhaps, if we read it as it is written, the story of a haunting told by observers who themselves, like the reader, are half in, half out of the ghost world but wholly of the physical one.

Realism in *Wuthering Heights*

Barbara Hardy

Despite its inclusion of fantastic and supernatural events, Barbara Hardy contends that *Wuthering Heights* is a realistic novel. Hardy, a professor of English language and literature at Royal Holloway College, University of London, writes that Brontë controls the supernatural elements of the novel by placing them in the context of ordinary details of routine life. The very real love of Catherine and Heathcliff, along with the presence of Brontë's narrators, also helps contribute to the "emotional vividness" and "dramatic truth," or realism, of the novel.

[*Wuthering Heights*] is not a fantasy where supernatural or mysterious events and causes move freely in and out of the action, distorting the appearances of the solid material world and the solid rational explanations. From the beginning we have seen the irrational passions and the supernatural suggestions controlled in this way by being placed in the context of 'normal' commonsense and familiar objects and routine. Even if we learn, as I believe we should, not to rely too securely on the rational explanations of Lockwood and the rational though slightly more superstitious responses of Nelly Dean, there is no doubt that what we may call the realism of the novel owes much to their presence. They are ordinary and familiar. They form a plausible bridge between the reader and the story of 'another species' which lies at the novel's heart. . . .

Wuthering Heights has the realism of its emotional vividness, not merely as shown in the 'dramatic truth' of Catherine and Heathcliff's wild passions and strange history, but also as shown in the dramatic truth of the other characters. The strange history is framed in the ordinary world inhab-

Reprinted from *Wuthering Heights* (*Emily Brontë*), by Barbara Hardy (Oxford: Blackwell, 1963) by permission of the author.

ited by Hareton and Catherine, victims of the strangeness and wildness but eventually emerging to lead their ordinary lives. It is framed too, as we have seen, in the point of view of Lockwood and Nelly Dean.

At the end we see Hareton and the second Catherine walking unafraid on the moors, just as Lockwood is unafraid even though he is visiting the churchyard at night—he who began by dreaming of ghosts. The familiar ordinary impression made, even if not conclusively, at the end of the novel, owes much not only to the impression these characters have made throughout the novel, but also to the natural setting and its solidity. It is in stormy winter that people are afraid in *Wuthering Heights* and the peaceful appearances at the end are the appearances of summer. Lockwood prefers the moors in summer, of course, and the last reassuring words rely significantly on hints of the seasons' limitations. The 'autumn storms' are yet to come, the heath and harebells are a part of the transient foliage, the wind will not always be soft, and the moths will stop their fluttering. But if the whole novel is still vibrating in our mind, we will be aware of the double implications of such a landscape. After all, we began in storm. After all, we do not know whether or not Heathcliff's dust is mingling with Catherine's beneath the quiet earth in final assertion of their defiance of death and religious rites. The 'any one' who *is* in a position to 'imagine unquiet slumbers for the sleepers in that quiet earth' might well be the reader of the novel. But the point I want to stress here is that the reader is throughout presented not only with the wild history but with the soberness of ordinary people and real nature. A novel which concentrated more purely on the passions and mysteries of Heathcliff and his Catherine would be more romantically remote from ordinary life. It would leave out the range of human experience which includes the spectators, like Lockwood and Nelly, or the peaceful and fortunate, like Hareton and Catherine. It would leave out the views of such ordinary people which form the medium for the strange history, a medium which both holds it at a distance and allows us to make up our own minds about its meaning and values. But it would also leave out a great deal within that strange history itself. . . .

REAL LOVE IN A REAL WORLD

Charlotte Brontë, in her second Preface to *Wuthering Heights*, tells us that without Heathcliff's feeling for Hareton

and Nelly we would not see him as a human being, but 'say
he was child neither of Lascar nor gipsy, but a man's shape
animated by demon life—a Ghoul—an Afreet'. It is a pity that
Charlotte does not say something about Catherine as well as
Heathcliff, and her comment that his love for Catherine 'is a
sentiment fierce and inhuman' is one you should think hard
about, since it seems at least open to argument. But it is generally true, I think, that Heathcliff and Catherine are made
real by their relationships with other characters and with
their environment.

Think of that early Christmas party, where Nelly watches
Catherine's conflict between her delight in her grand new
friends and her love for the disgraced Heathcliff, as she puts
up some show of eating her dinner. Think of the earlier
scene where Heathcliff and Catherine gaze through the window of Thrushcross Grange at the 'splendid place carpeted
with crimson' and the Linton children quarreling over their
dog. Or the scene where Catherine returns from her stay at
the Grange, in elegant ringlets and the new dress which is
both a slightly self-conscious pleasure and a barrier between her and the dogs, the dirty Heathcliff, and even Nelly
Dean, 'all flour making the Christmas cake'. All these scenes
are socially and visually real and solid. We see the uphol-
stery, the drops and chains of the chandelier, the enchanted
vision for the two wild children from the Heights. The characters inhabit the real world of places, things, and activity.
Nelly Dean does her dusting while Edgar Linton gets his
first taste of Catherine's temper. Heathcliff decides to be a
good boy and asks Nelly to make him clean and tidy. And
this solid environment continues throughout the novel. Isabella makes lumpy porridge on her first inauspicious return from her elopement with Heathcliff. Nelly worries because Heathcliff is not eating his meals, and it is real food
which he accepts and then is forced to neglect. . . . The characters are shown in relationship with Nelly's solid ordinari-
ness, and an important aspect of this kind of realism is the
solid portrayal of environment too.

ORDINARY DETAILS

Natural details, as well as social and domestic ones, play
their part. Consider the moving moment when Nelly goes
out, after Catherine's death, to find Heathcliff standing under the ash-tree: 'He had been standing a long time in that

position, for I saw a pair of ousels passing and repassing scarcely three feet from him, busy in building their nest, and regarding his proximity no more than a piece of timber'. Heathcliff's 'knowledge' of the death is tethered to this ordinary detail. It is given substance and made more moving by the detail and its implications.

Consider the wild and hysterical scene when Catherine pulls her pillow to pieces and arranges the feathers on the sheet:

> 'That's a turkey's' she murmured to herself; 'and this is a wild duck's; and this is a pigeon's. Ah, they put pigeon's feathers in the pillows—no wonder I couldn't die! Let me take care to throw it on the floor when I lie down. And here is a moorcock's; and this—I should know it among a thousand—it's a lapwing's. Bonny bird; wheeling over our heads in the middle of the moor. It wanted to get to its nest, for the clouds had touched the swells, and it felt rain coming. This feather was picked up from the heath, the bird was not shot: we saw its nest in the winter, full of little skeletons. Heathcliff set a trap over it, and the old ones dare not come. I made him promise he'd never shoot a lapwing after that, and he didn't. Yes, here are more! Did he shoot my lapwings, Nelly? Are they red, any of them! Let me look.'

In many ways this is a wild strange speech, rather like Ophelia's flower speech in *Hamlet* in being both fey and precise. Nelly is frightened and answers, as commonsense usually does, by telling Catherine to pull herself together: 'Give over with that baby-work!' But the speech is a fine example of Emily Brontë's realism as well as of her ability to delineate abnormal states of consciousness. The trap and the little skeletons have a sinister reference to the future as well as the past, but they are more than a symbol. They are a part of actual things and experiences and places: the disturbed mind lovingly identifies the real feathers, and the recognition brings with it real memories. When we think of Heathcliff as a diabolical figure, or even as a man whose love for Catherine is 'fierce and inhuman' we forget such details as this, which create the world of childish joys and companionship in which this love grew up. When a little later, Catherine tells Nelly of her hallucination of grief and misery in which the last seven years 'grew a blank' and she returned to the misery of her separation from Heathcliff we have a bare and violent strained expression of emotion. It is the small solid details, natural or domestic, like the feathers or the flour on Nelly's hands, that make the love seem human and recogniseable at least in origin. Nelly's response, . . . gives us the sense of ordinary relationships so that Catherine and Heathcliff are not seen entirely in isolation, as belonging to 'another species', but it is the scenes and objects, as well as the people, which contribute to the feeling that the strange passions and events take place in a familiar landscape.

So that when we come to the last description of the three graves we have already become solidly habituated to the rhythm of the seasons, both in actual description and in the imagery used by the characters. The natural setting, as I have suggested earlier, is not a mere set of symbols. It has fo-

LYRICISM AND RESERVE

Muriel Spark and Derek Stanford suggest that the "poetic realism" of Brontë's style presents itself in her lyricism and reserve. Lyricism is evident in the spontaneous natures of Catherine and her daughter, and reserve derives from the "dourness" of Nelly and Joseph.

I [contend that] the poetic realism of Emily's style [resides] in a combination of lyricism and reserve. These opposite traits are brought together in artistic conjunction most naturally by Emily; and it is the play of these characteristics that makes for the genuine tone of the novel. Without the lyrical element present, the notes of dourness and reserve would leave *Wuthering Heights* a pedestrian chronicle of cruelties committed in a brutish district, and with little in it to redeem the story. Similarly, without the reserve, the lyricism would want conviction. Lockwood's nightmare, Heathcliff's obsession, Catherine's delirium and ghostly reappearance: these, by themselves, would be too much if *Wuthering Heights* was to have avoided the fate of being just another Gothic novel. Then, too, the environment is such that *Wuthering Heights* might have become a simple idyll of the soil, with the regional interest as the chief factor. The "unreclaimed" nature of this "remote region" is certainly one of the charms of the book. The wildness and remoteness is well suggested when we learn that, although the Earnshaws live on a farm, they lack even such rustic luxuries as apples and pears. In fact these fruits are looked upon as novelties, for when the elder Mr. Earnshaw sets out on his sixty-mile tramp to Liverpool, he promises Nelly Dean he will bring her a pocketful back with him.

Muriel Spark and Derek Stanford, "Chapter X: Spirit, Style, and Values," *Emily Brontë: Her Life and Work.* New York: London House and Maxwell, 1960, pp. 260–262.

liage which changes, creatures which move, weather which shifts. At few points in the novel—not even in the wildest accounts of delirium and passion and anguish—can we say that there is no link with the ordinary world. We have to except the dreams, and these are frankly present as dreams. The few sinister crannies I mentioned, through which suggestion leaks which cannot be always rationally answered, are the more frightening and moving because they are cracks in a recognisable and solid world. If *Wuthering Heights* is one of the strangest and most poetic of novels, it is not an unrealistic story.

CHAPTER 3

Psychological Issues in *Wuthering Heights*

READINGS ON
WUTHERING HEIGHTS

Heathcliff's Monomania

Graeme Tytler

Graeme Tytler of Southeastern Louisiana University writes that the references to monomania in *Wuthering Heights* describe a mental illness common in medical texts of Brontë's era. Heathcliff displays symptoms of this "disease of sensibility" in his obsessive love of Cathy and in his need for power and revenge. Despite Heathcliff's hallucinations and sleeplessness, his need to confess his sufferings, his frequent rapid breathing, hollow cheeks, and bloodshot eyes—all symptoms of monomania—he is never diagnosed mentally ill by those around him. Tytler explains that because Heathcliff remains lucid and seemingly rational, his illness goes untreated, as did the illnesses of many monomaniacs in Brontë's day.

When Nelly Dean has recalled how, in bewildered incomprehension, she interrupted Heathcliff's second long confession about Cathy's haunting of him to ask what he meant a few moments earlier by speaking of "a strange change approaching", she goes on to intimate that he "might have had a monomania on the subject of his departed idol". For the present-day reader, 'monomania' is usually synonymous with 'craze', 'fad', 'obsession', 'hobbyhorse', and the like, as, indeed, it was for a good many people in the mid-nineteenth century, including novelists. Yet 'monomania' originally denoted a type of mental illness, and had often been used in that sense in medical writings by the time *Wuthering Heights* appeared in 1847. That Emily Brontë intends 'monomania' in its clinical sense is suggested by the realistic detail with which she depicts not only Heathcliff's illness, but also its counterpart, namely, Cathy's 'brain fever', which, like monomania, was a common, not to say fashionable, disease in both life and literature. . . .

Excerpted from Graeme Tytler, "Heathcliff's Monomania: An Anachronism in *Wuthering Heights*, Brontë Society *Transactions*, vol. 20, no. 6 (1962), pp. 331–43. Reprinted by permission of the publisher.

It is probable that Emily Brontë was aware of monomania from her assiduous reading of national periodicals, or even her knowledge of the York Retreat, which was famous in her day for the humane treatment of insanity, and through her knowledge that George Nussey (the brother of Charlotte's friend Ellen) was, to the family's great distress, being treated for mental illness in a private asylum in York. Postulating that Emily Brontë intends the word 'monomania' in its clinical sense, let us consider how far her presentation of Heathcliff can be deemed an expression of a true knowledge of that illness.

The fact that [Jean-Etienne-Dominique] Esquirol [one of the founders of modern psychiatry] regarded monomania first and foremost as "the disease of advancing civilization", or, more specifically, the disease of the rising bourgeoisie, with its determined quest for self-fulfilment, already has some relevance to our image of Heathcliff as a man who, through relentless effort, raises himself above his social limitations and achieves conspicuous material success. Relevant, too, is Esquirol's definition of monomania as "the disease of going to extremes, of singularization, of one-sidedness" when we think of Heathcliff's obsession with power, domination and revenge. Much more significant for our purposes, however, are Esquirol's following remarks on the causes of monomania: "Monomania is essentially a disease of the sensibility. It reposes altogether upon the affections, and its study is inseparable from a knowledge of the passions. Its seat is in the heart of man, and it is there that we must search for it, in order to possess ourselves of all its peculiarities. How many are the cases of monomania caused by thwarted love, by fear, vanity, wounded self-love, or disappointed ambition." Such words forcibly remind us of Heathcliff's tragic relationship with Cathy, and it is in their light that we should now examine it in some detail.

HEATHCLIFF'S OBSESSION

Heathcliff's love for Cathy is more or less an obsession, which seems to have begun before he leaves the Heights on the evening of her betrothal to Edgar. That the obsession has continued during Heathcliff's three-year absence is evident when, on the night of his return, he says to Cathy: "I've fought through a bitter life since I last heard your voice, and you must forgive me, for I struggled only for you!" Heath-

cliff's obsession with Cathy is apparent even after his marriage to Isabella, to the extent that he begins to exhibit abnormal behaviour. Thus Isabella asks in her letter to Nelly:
"Is Heathcliff a man? If so, is he mad? And if not, is he a
devil?"; and, after her escape from the Heights, she describes
him as "a monster" and "not a human being". Nelly herself
is disconcerted by Heathcliff's way of disparaging Isabella,
which she condemns as "the talk of a madman". Even in his
final meeting with Cathy, Heathcliff's vehemence of language and violence of physical contact seem abnormal.
Thus he says to Cathy: "Don't torture me till I'm as mad as
yourself", at the same time as Nelly notices him "grinding
his teeth". Abnormal, too, is the rage behind Heathcliff's
apostrophising the dead Cathy because she has failed to
mention him by name on her deathbed, his bidding her to
haunt him, his dashing his head "against the knotted trunk",
and his crying out "like a savage beast getting goaded to
death with knives and spears". Then, Heathcliff's talk of suicide, as connected with Cathy, also has to be taken into account when judging him as a potential monomaniac. Most
important of all, however, is his determination to remain in
some sort of relationship with Cathy after her death, for it is
in that very single-minded determination that lie the roots of
his monomania.

   If, as the foregoing suggests, Heathcliff seems to show a
certain predisposition to insanity up to the time of Cathy's
death, and just beyond, it is not until some eighteen years
later that he begins to exhibit signs of mental illness. A good
deal of Heathcliff's talk and behaviour from Chapter XXIX
onwards may, for example, be considered essentially symp-
tomatic of monomania—the hallucinations, the sleeplessness, the talking to himself or to Cathy's ghost, the distrac-
tion in company, the sighs and groans, even the cruelty to
Catherine and Linton, all of which can be matched with
monomania nosology and case histories. Whether Heathcliff's rapid breathing, hollow cheeks or bloodshot eyes, as
observed and commented on by Nelly in the last few days of
his life, are also peculiar to monomaniacs cannot be said for
certain, since Esquirol and others say relatively little about
the physical effects of the illness. However, when some five
days before Heathcliff's death, Nelly keeps referring to his
eyes with phrases such as "a strange joyful glitter", "the
same unnatural . . . appearance of joy", "glittering restless

eyes", and so on, we are reminded of Esquirol's following words: "The physiognomy of the monomaniac is animated, changeable, pleased: the eyes are lively and brilliant." It is also interesting to reflect on the extent to which Nelly's detailed account of the five days leading up to Heathcliff's sudden death seems to bear out Esquirol's experience that "the progress of monomania is rapid and violent" and that "its termination is often unexpected".

That Heathcliff's mental illness is, above all, an obsessional disorder characteristic of monomania is strikingly evident in those passages where he confesses to being relentlessly haunted by Cathy's image. This is suggested, for instance, in Chapter XXXI when Lockwood, on his third visit to the Heights, overhears Heathcliff muttering to himself about Hareton's resemblance to Cathy: "How the devil is he so like? I can hardly bear to see him." It is also significant that Lockwood immediately afterwards notices "a restless, anxious expression in his countenance" which he has "never remarked there before", for his words indicate that Heathcliff's illness has now become acute. In other episodes, Emily Brontë underlines the acuteness of Heathcliff's condition by the way in which he is shown to be daunted by Catherine's resemblance to her mother, especially in those moments when she defies his tyrannous domination, and, more particularly, when he detects, probably for the first time, the close resemblance between Catherine and Hareton, as if that resemblance once and for all confirmed the terrible power exercised over him by Cathy, not to say the ultimate triumph of the Earnshaws. Shortly afterwards, in his second long confession to Nelly, Heathcliff makes it abundantly clear that his obsessional disorder has reached a point where Cathy has become an ineluctable physiognomical presence. Thus having dismissed Hareton's "startling likeness to Catherine" and its fearful connection with Cathy as being "the least [potent] to arrest [his] imagination", Heathcliff continues:

> . . . for what is not connected with her for me? And what does not recall her? I cannot look down to the floor, but her features are shaped in the flags! In every cloud, in every tree—filling the air at night, and caught by glimpses in every object, by day I am surrounded with her image! The entire world is a dreadful collection of memoranda that she did exist, and that I have lost her.

HEATHCLIFF'S CONFESSIONS

In this connection, it is interesting to note that the author seems to be hinting at monomania on both the occasions when Heathcliff speaks to Nelly at length about his sufferings with Cathy. Indeed, just as on the earlier occasion, Nelly has observed how, at the end of his long account, Heathcliff's eyebrows imparted "a peculiar look of trouble and a painful appearance of mental tension towards *one absorbing subject*" (italics mine), so on this occasion, some seven months later, Heathcliff seems to point up his monomaniacal state when he says to Nelly: ". . . it is by compulsion that I do the slightest act, not prompted by *one thought*, and by compulsion that I notice anything dead or alive, which is not associated with *one universal idea*" (italics mine). The authenticity of Heathcliff's monomania is also corroborated by the fact that, rather like those mental patients interviewed by Esquirol and his associates, Heathcliff has been driven to make his confessions to someone he can confide in, so as to seek relief from his unbearable sufferings. As he says to Nelly in the middle of his second confession: "But you'll not talk of what I tell you, and my mind is so eternally secluded in itself, it is tempting to turn it over to another."

But despite all the evidence to suggest that Heathcliff does, indeed, end his days as a monomaniac, the question may, nevertheless, arise as to whether the term 'monomania', albeit used tentatively by Nelly, and only in retrospect, can be said properly to describe his illness. The question is not an idle one, all the more as Nelly herself, though often privy to Heathcliff's bizarre talk and behaviour, is never quite convinced that he is really mentally ill. And yet Nelly's unawareness in this respect is, oddly enough, the very thing that happens to justify her use of the word 'monomania', for monomania was, in fact, an illness that tended to remain hidden from all but the most expert eyes, and not least because its victims tended to remain in normal physical health. That may explain why a simple country doctor like Kenneth, though quite cognisant of the dangers of insanity inherent in the delirious fevers he diagnoses in Cathy, but otherwise probably unfamiliar with the latest developments in psychological medicine, should also have been deceived by Heathcliff's good health enough to be, as Nelly recalls, "perplexed to pronounce of what disorder the master died".

HEATHCLIFF IS THE DEVIL

Sheila Smith writes that many of the descriptions of Heathcliff throughout the novel associate him with evil.

The first description of Heathcliff in the novel associates him with the Devil. Mr Earnshaw, setting down the ragged bundle scooped up from the Liverpool slums, says to his wife: '"you must e'en take it as a gift of God, though it's as dark almost as if it came from the devil"'. The diabolical references continue throughout the novel. Nelly comments on Hindley's degradation of Heathcliff after Mr Earnshaw's death: 'His treatment of [Heathcliff] was enough to make a fiend of a saint. And, truly, it appeared as if the lad *were* possessed of something diabolical at that period . . . I could not half tell what an infernal house we had'. When Catherine discovers Isabella's infatuation with Heathcliff, she teasingly offers her to him as a wife, and then withdraws, saying '"It is as bad as offering Satan a lost soul— Your bliss lies, like his, in inflicting misery"'. Isabella elopes with Heathcliff and writes to Nelly after the honeymoon, making explicit the hitherto implicit question: '"Is Mr Heathcliff a man? If so, is he mad? And if not, is he a devil?"' When Isabella escapes from the Heights to the Grange she feels '"blest as a soul escaped from purgatory"'. So when Heathcliff utters 'a fiendish laugh' at the idea that he has both degraded Hindley's son Hareton and made him love him, the accumulation of satanic references and the context remove the phrase from the world of melodramatic villains, and give it the emotional charge of the source of evil. Young Cathy's imprisonment at the Heights so that she shall marry Linton and thus, at his approaching death, secure Edgar Linton's and Isabella's property to Heathcliff does, largely by the insistent use of diabolical references, have the imaginative associations of evil enchantment, and 'possession' in both the literal and diabolical senses. The darkness associated with Heathcliff—complexion, eyes, mood, deeds, even clothes—grows to a terrifying intensity until he seems to have supernatural powers of control. He exerts the fear of the Devil over Linton, and likens the terror to the effect of a ghost: '"I fancy he sees me often, though I am not near. Hareton says he wakes and shrieks in the night by the hour together; and calls you [Cathy] to protect him from me"'. As in the description of Lockwood's nightmare, psychological states here are convincingly described in supernatural terms, and the supernatural refers to an area of experience assumed to be part of 'reality'.

Sheila Smith, "'At Once Strong and Eerie': The Supernatural in *Wuthering Heights* and Its Debt to the Traditional Ballad," *Review of English Studies*, vol. 43, no. 172, November 1992, pp. 511–12.

It may also explain why Nelly, herself deceived by her assumption that Heathcliff is "quite strong and healthy" and by his confidence that that good health will enable him to live to a great old age, should make this comment after reporting his second long confession: "Though he seldom before had revealed this state of mind, even by looks, it was his habitual mood, I had no doubt: he asserted it himself—but not a soul, from his general bearing, would have conjectured the fact. You did not, when you saw him, Mr Lockwood."

HEATHCLIFF'S DECEPTIVE ILLNESS

Nelly's latter utterance, presumptuous as it may seem, is, however, quite valid inasmuch as, notwithstanding Heathcliff's strange behaviour in the oak-panelled room, Lockwood nowhere appears to question his sanity. What is the reason for this? It will be remembered that when Lockwood first visits the Heights, his initial impression of Heathcliff—and probably the reader's—is of a normal, if somewhat morose, country gentleman, whose normality is manifest partly through the more or less light-hearted way in which he reacts to his tenant's fight with the dogs and partly through his efforts to be hospitable to him afterwards. In the eyes of Lockwood, the eighteenth-century man of reason and intellect par excellence, Heathcliff is evidently a godsend in that cultural desert, for he makes a special point of noting in his diary that, having introduced "a subject of conversation that might be of interest to [his tenant]," namely, "a discussion on the advantages and disadvantages of [Lockwood's] present place of retirement," Heathcliff proved "very intelligent on the topics [they] touched"—intelligent enough, it seems, for the tenant to "volunteer another visit" the following day. And if on that volunteered visit Heathcliff at first exhibits the same moroseness as before, his conversation remains, nevertheless, essentially rational, to the extent that he even manages to entrap his talkative guest in a kind of game of logic by keeping him guessing as to how the members of the household are inter-related.

The interest of Lockwood's first two meetings with Heathcliff, however, is that they bear out the experience of practically all those who, whether laymen or experts, found themselves in the company of a monomaniac without realizing it. In this connection, it is noteworthy that Esquirol, Prichard, Linas and others assert the difficulty of recognizing mono-

maniacs precisely because, apart from their specific partial
manias, they could reason correctly, logically and coherently, and, in some instances, displayed the highest intellectual powers. That is why readers of *Wuthering Heights*,
themselves confident of Heathcliff's intelligence and good
sense at the outset, are no less astonished than Lockwood at
his nervous behaviour on his entry into the oak-panelled
room, and at the humourless incomprehension and eccentric manner with which he responds to Lockwood's com-
plaints about the room being haunted and "swarming with
ghosts and goblins". Thus, instead of laughing off Lockwood's explanations of his nightmares as he might have
done, say, at the evening meal, Heathcliff reacts in a curi-
ously distracted, even distraught, manner. There is also
something utterly abnormal about Heathcliff's "crushing his
nails into his palms, and grinding his teeth to subdue the
maxillary convulsions" and striking his forehead "with
rage". When, in answer to Lockwood's account of spelling
the name Catherine in order to help him to sleep, Heathcliff
exclaims, "God, he's mad to speak so", we cannot help judging Lockwood's explanation of his nightmares to be perfectly
reasonable, but Heathcliff's talk and behaviour, on the other
hand, to be close to unreason. What we do not realize at the
time, any more than Lockwood does, is that Heathcliff is,
presumably, having a severe fit of monomania. Even though
Lockwood sees Heathcliff climbing onto the bed and calling
out to Cathy's ghost in "a gush of grief", he still seems reluctant to take that curious behaviour any more seriously
than he did his own irrational utterances about his nightmares, in that he merely dismisses it as "a piece of superstition which belied, oddly, his apparent sense" and then declares that "[his] compassion made [him] overlook its folly".
Moreover, in his determination to classify Heathcliff as a
sort of *alter ego* of like rationality and intellect, Lockwood is
probably reassured, not only by finding him an hour or two
later in the kitchen acting as normally, if as grimly, as on the
previous day, but, more particularly, by being able to record
that, on a visit to the Grange a month later, Heathcliff was
"charitable enough" to sit at his sick bedside and "talk on
some other subjects than pills, and draughts, blisters and
leeches". Nor, when visiting Heathcliff for the third and last
time at the Heights, does Lockwood seem to attach much importance to the latter's being "sparer in person", or mutter-

ing to himself about Hareton's resemblance to Cathy, perhaps because in his bid to retain his image of Heathcliff's rationality, he allows himself to be deceived by the bluff manner with which the latter responds to the news of his
imminent departure and then teases him with a warning not
to try to get out of paying his rent.

Lockwood's apparent failure to recognize the clinical implications of the contradictions in Heathcliff's personality
and behaviour, then, may be adjudged quite typical of a good
many ordinary people confronted by a monomaniac in the
nineteenth century. The same is also true of Nelly's own failure to understand Heathcliff's illness, except that she is, of
course, never witness to anything like the behaviour he exhibits in the oak-panelled room. Like Lockwood, Nelly is especially deceived by Heathcliff's rationality and mental
alertness on several occasions. Even when Heathcliff's
monomania seems to be at its most acute, Nelly recalls, for
instance, that, while conversing with Joseph one morning
about some farming business, he "turned his head continu-
ally aside, and had the same exalted expression, even more
exaggerated", but, nevertheless, "gave clear, minute direc-
tions concerning the matter discussed". The fact that Heathcliff can, moreover, speak quite lucidly and coherently about
his mental state, as we see, for example, when having said
that his confessions have not relieved him, but that they
"may account for some otherwise unaccountable phases of
humour which [he] show[s]", is interesting in the light of
claims made by Esquirol and others about the rationality
with which monomaniacs can talk about themselves and
their condition. It is, therefore, little wonder that, despite being "alarmed at his manner" during his second confession,
Nelly should have been certain that Heathcliff was "neither
in danger of losing his senses nor dying". Thus we see how,
through this constant emphasis on Heathcliff's intelligence
and rationality, even during his worst mental crises, Emily
Brontë not only justifies her use of 'monomania', but also
confirms the authenticity as well as the dramatic skill with
which she has delineated the illness in her novel.

The Incest Taboo in *Wuthering Heights*

Kathryn B. McGuire

Raised as brother and sister, Heathcliff and Cathy are forbidden, in life, from marrying or otherwise expressing the extent of their passionate love. Kathryn B. McGuire, of the Department of English at the University of North Texas at Denton, explores the dynamics of their incestuous desires. Characteristic of incest, the guilt from these taboo desires, McGuire says, is manifest in Heathcliff's vampiristic and necrophilic tendencies and his drive for power. Cathy responds with fevers, fits, and delirium. The two remain obsessed, tormented, and in Heathcliff's case haunted, until they are finally coupled in death.

The brooding atmosphere of Wuthering Heights, the intense characters, and the disturbing theme lure the reader into a world at once repelling and seductive. Who or what is the mysterious Heathcliff? Why does the mutual passion between Cathy Earnshaw and him remain unrequited when there is no apparent obstacle to their union? Why is their consuming physical attachment superseded by a morbid fascination with union after death? I propose that an unconscious incest taboo impeded the two lovers' expectations of normal sexual union and led them to spiritualize their attachment, eventually leading them to believe that they could find union only after death.

Criticism of *Wuthering Heights* has characteristically taken one of two approaches when the question of incest has been raised. Some critics have suggested that Heathcliff was the illegitimate son of Mr. Earnshaw, but no textual evidence exists to support the hypothesis that Heathcliff and Cathy were blood brother and sister. In any case, for an incest taboo to exist, it is irrelevant whether Cathy and Heathcliff are blood

Adapted from Kathryn B. McGuire, "The Incest Taboo in *Wuthering Heights:* A Modern Appraisal," *American Imago*, vol. 45, no. 2 (Summer 1988), pp. 217–24. Copyright © 1988 by the Association for Applied Psychoanalysis, Inc. Reprinted by permission of The Johns Hopkins University Press.

relatives. What is essential is that they were *raised* as brother and sister. Heathcliff entered the family when he was seven and Cathy was six. They shared all living arrangements as brother and sister, including sleeping together. . . .

Central to a discussion of incest is an understanding of advancements in the study of the Oedipal complex. Modern psychologists, sociologists, and anthropologists maintain that incest can be viewed as an attempt by fragmented man to achieve wholeness and immortality. In a sense, incest offers the most nearly perfect way of attaining oneness, providing the metaphor of like with like merging into complete possession; by suppressing the sexual instincts, this possession can be based on the eternal union of the spirit. Yet incest, arising out of a need for integration, paradoxically results most often in the severest disintegration.

In cases of brother/sister incest, the siblings are likely to be products of an isolated, introverted upbringing. The environment in which Heathcliff and Cathy were raised was extraordinarily conducive to the development of an incestuous situation. Inhabitants of the lonely moors, "completely removed from the stir of society," the family circle was closed to all except the servants and a handful of neighbors who lived at some distance.

The role of isolation is significant in incest, as both a motive for the relationship and as an effect of its practice. Although incest arises from a yearning for completeness and belonging, it most often results in further alienation. The incestuous lover, rather than turning outward instead turns inward, a situation which can only end disastrously; in a sense he is attempting a kind of union with himself: Cathy came to believe "I *am* Heathcliff"; Heathcliff said, "I *cannot* live without my soul!"

VAMPIRES AND WEREWOLVES

The aberrant behavior of the two lovers, especially Heathcliff's vampiristic and necrophilic tendencies and Cathy's physical disorders, is recognized as characteristic of incest. Of course, any discussion of behavioral patterns which suggests an incestuous fixation must begin with Heathcliff, for it is he who best exemplifies the consequences of violating the incest taboo. . . .

The combination of Heathcliff's deprived early environment and his equally deprived adolescence indicates that he never received the kind of nurturing necessary to mature out of a symbiotic relationship. As a result, he spent much of his energy keeping unmet dependency needs out of aware-ness. He did this through sadistic behavior, at times border-ing on depravity and self-destruction.

Along with sadism, Heathcliff exhibited other bizarre traits which we, as modern readers, can understand in light of psychological breakthroughs in the study of incest. Psy-choanalyst Ernest Jones, in his book *On the Nightmare*, demonstrated empirically the relationship between incest, Satanism, vampirism, lycanthropy (or werewolfism), and necrophilia—all of which were manifested by Heathcliff. In folklore and myth, all of these disorders are considered de-monic, a predominant characteristic of Heathcliff. Critics have pointed out the dozens of passages in which he is re-ferred to as "fiend," "ghoul," "devil," etc., but there are also many allusions to vampirism in general and two of its spe-cific forms, lycanthropy and necrophilia.

Strictly speaking, Heathcliff was not a vampire, for the term designates a re-animated body or soul of a dead person who sucks the blood from the living in order to draw him into death, the vampire himself being reanimated in the process. But the predominant imagery of vampirism throughout the novel is so pervasive that it seems fair to say that Brontë created at least a metaphorical vampire. Jones demonstrated that the incest complex underlies the vampire one; he makes a parallel between the vampire who sucks blood to sustain himself and the infant who receives life-sustaining nourishment from the mother's breast. The whole superstition of vampirism, according to Jones, is "shot through with the theme of guilt" which is generated in the incest conflicts in infancy.

Jones pointed out that the relationship between the were-wolf (lycanthrope) and the vampire superstitions are closely connected. In many parts of the world the idea is prevalent that "werewolves become vampires after their death." From the blood-sucking of one to the ravenous lust of the other is but a small step.

Images of both vampirism and lycanthropy abound in the novel in regard to Heathcliff's appearance, as well as his be-havior. According to folklore, "Werewolves could be recog-nized when in human form by having heavy eyebrows that met together. . . ." Nelly described Heathcliff as having "thick

brows, that instead of rising arched, sink in the middle."
When he arrived at Wuthering Heights, Nelly tells how he
spoke some "gibberish that nobody could understand," even
though he must have been seven years old. By sixteen he had
"acquired a slouching gait, and ignoble look," and he had
"sharp cannibal teeth." Cathy told Isabella that he was a
"fierce, pitiless, wolfish man," who would "seize and devour
her up."

The manifestations of vampirism in general and lycanthropy in particular heightened as Cathy neared death.
Heathcliff, in his own words, "haunted" the Grange garden
every night for six hours. Nelly reveals his behavior during
Cathy's final hours: he "gnashed" and "foamed like a mad
dog" until Nelly felt as if she were not "in the company of
[her] own species; it appeared that he would not understand,
though [she] spoke to him." After Cathy's death, he "howled,
not like a man, but like a savage beast getting goaded to
death with knives and spears," and Nelly "observed several
splashes of blood about the bark of the tree, and his hands
and forehead were both stained."

A STRANGE DESIRE

Heathcliff manifested the symptoms of necrophilia immediately after Cathy's death. Necrophilia is another sexual aber-
ration which, like vampirism, arises from incestuous desires
and guilt. Jones explains that the necrophiliac believes that
"a dead person who loves will love forever and will never be
weary of giving and receiving caresses." This fantasy particularly appealed to Heathcliff, for "the relationship has none
of the inconvenient consequences that sexuality may bring
in its train in life." In other words, Heathcliff would violate
no incest taboo by dreaming of "sleeping the last sleep by
that sleeper," with his "cheek frozen against hers."

Nelly discloses Heathcliff's necrophilic tendencies; she
reveals that he visited Cathy's funeral chamber at night, a
fact that she realized because of the "disarrangement of the
drapery about the corpse's face." We learn from Isabella that
he slept on Cathy's grave during the summer months. We
later discover from Heathcliff himself that the night of
Cathy's burial he had attempted to remove the dirt from her
coffin, but as he bent over the grave he seemed to sense her
presence "not under [him], but on the earth." The sense of
relief caused him to re-cover the grave and return home. All

HEATHCLIFF IS EARNSHAW'S ILLEGITIMATE SON

Eric Solomon points to Heathcliff's sudden and ill-explained appearance in the Earnshaw family, as well as his insistent claim to Wuthering Heights, as evidence that he might be Earnshaw's illegitimate son.

[When Mr.] Earnshaw returns with a mysterious dirty child whom his wife "must e'en take as a gift of God." He gives a vague and illogical report of finding the homeless and starving child in the Liverpool gutters. Earnshaw's rationalization of the adoption seems weak:

> Not a soul knew to whom it belonged, he said, and his money and time, being both limited, he thought it better to take it home with him, at once, than run into vain expenses there; because he was determined he would not leave it as he found it.

. . . Mrs. Earnshaw considers her husband to be mad, and the narrator, tart Nelly Dean, expresses doubts through her manner of recounting the tale. She informs Lockwood that Earnshaw "*tried* to explain the matter; but he was *really* half dead with fatigue . . . all that I could make out . . . was *a tale* of his seeing it. . . ."

The brief picture of Mrs. Earnshaw presented here would certainly supply an added motive for concealment of a child who could possibly be Earnshaw's illegitimate offspring. She "was ready to fling it out of doors"; she grumbles and berates the exhausted traveler. How would such a woman have reacted to any honest admission of sinful adultery? Earnshaw could only bring a by-blow into the family by devious means, as long as his wife was still alive.

In addition, Heathcliff soon becomes Earnshaw's favorite, more cherished than his own children, an unnatural occurrence surely—unless this is a natural child. Nelly has her suspicions. Earnshaw, she comments, "took to the child *strangely*," this "poor, fatherless child, as *he* called him." Hindley, for his part, sees Heathcliff "as a usurper of his parent's affections.". . .

Certainly *Wuthering Heights* can be read without any such theory of Heathcliff's birth. Yet this view supplies an answer to some of the novel's ambiguities. If Heathcliff and Cathy were—even unknowingly—brother and sister, they obviously never could marry on earth, however violent their passion might be. . . . Again, Heathcliff, as Earnshaw's real son, would have an increased motivation for his bitter insistence that Wuthering Heights must belong to him.

Eric Solomon, "The Incest Theme in *Wuthering Heights*," *Nineteenth-Century Fiction*, vol. 14, 1959–1960, pp. 80–83.

the way back, he "could *almost* see her, and yet [he] *could not.*" After that he continued to be tortured by the feeling of her presence, yet the inability to see her.

Jones explained this insatiable desire to be revisited by the dead as mostly a "mechanism of identification." He maintained that "the deepest source of this projection is doubtless to be found in the wish that ultimately springs from childhood memories of being left alone by the loved parent."

THE LUST FOR POWER

Likewise, the insistence on complete possession is, according to Jones, "particularly urgent with those who have not succeeded in emancipating themselves from the infantile desire to make a test case of their first love problem, that of incest with the mother and rivalry with the father."

Of course, rivalry with the father is a primary manifestation of the incest fixation. Nowhere is this rivalry more apparent than in the relationship between Heathcliff and Hindley, a relationship which illustrates Freud's explanation of the incest taboo, the Myth of the Primal Horde. According to Freud, patricide and incest were the only two crimes which troubled primitive society. In the myth, the brothers killed the father because he "stood so powerfully in the way of their sexual demands and their desire for power." The incest taboo originated as a result of the guilt which then overwhelmed them.

Freud's myth of the father slain by the sons because they lusted for his power and his mate provides a basis for the consequences of revenge and death which follow in the wake of incest. . . . The details of Hindley's death approximately one year after Heathcliff returned from his three-year sojourn are recounted by Nelly in such a way as to imply that Heathcliff could have murdered him.

Suspicion surrounding Hindley's death is planted in the reader's mind by Nelly, whose first thought upon hearing of the death was "Had he fair play?" She hastened to Wuthering Heights to learn from Heathcliff that Hindley had deliberately drunk himself to death. Nelly seemed unconvinced of Heathcliff's innocence, however, saying that his deportment "expressed a flinty gratification at a piece of difficult work, successfully executed" and that there was "something like exultation in his aspect" when the body was being removed. . . .

Cathy's Fevers, Fits, and Delirium

At the inception of Cathy's attachment to Heathcliff, she acted as a kind of surrogate mother to him and is portrayed in terms which suggest a maternal superiority. When she was separated from him, however, she easily lost that superiority and reacted in child-like fashion, throwing tantrums, obstinately refusing to take shelter from the elements, refusing to eat, having appalling nightmares, and threatening self-destruction.

Just as Heathcliff consistently rejected his instinctual self, so did Cathy. Whereas Heathcliff's repressed sexuality surfaced in a number of bizarre behavioral traits, Cathy's emerged as a variety of physical and mental disorders. She suffered a succession of illnesses, variously referred to as "delirium," "a fever," a "kind of fit," "brain fever," and severe headaches. In fact, every time that Cathy was physically separated from Heathcliff, she became physically ill, most seriously on the occasions which threatened total separation.

For example, we learn through Lockwood's reading of Cathy's diary and through Nelly's account of Cathy's delirium just prior to her death that Cathy's headaches and "temporary derangement" occur when Hindley banished Heathcliff from Cathy's bedroom at ages thirteen and twelve respectively. The text is unclear whether they actually shared the same bed, although Cathy's statement. "I was laid alone for the first time," certainly leaves room for that conjecture. Nevertheless, they at least shared the same room, apparently just the two of them for the three years that Hindley was away at college.

Of course, the most sensational example of this repression is Cathy's second hysterical attack, which eventually led to her death. Once again, the attack occurred because she was separated from Heathcliff, for Edgar had just barred Heathcliff from Thrushcross Grange. The doctor, Kenneth, commented that he could not "help fancying there's an extra cause for this [her hysteria]."

In addition to sharing Heathcliff's repressive tendencies, Cathy was indirectly given a share of his vampiristic tendencies. She asked Nelly, "Who is to separate us [Heathcliff and her], pray? They'll meet the fate of Milo!" Milo, according to a textual note, was a "Greek athlete who, when trying to rend a tree asunder, was trapped in the cliff and eaten by wolves." When Edgar tried to force her to choose between Heathcliff and him, she is described in vampiristic terms as "dashing her head against the arm of the sofa, and grinding her teeth, so that you might fancy she would crash them to splinters!" Nelly further described her reaction to separation from Heathcliff: "She stretched herself out still and turned up her eyes, while her cheeks, at once blanched and livid assumed the aspect of death. . . . 'She has blood on her lips!' [Edgar] said, shuddering." This description is suggestive of Heathcliff when he learned of Cathy's death. The vampiristic image is evident as Nelly continues: "She started up—her hair flying over her shoulders, her eyes flashing, the muscles of her neck and arms standing out preternaturally." Her appearance as she neared death furthered the image: "Her present countenance had a wild vindictiveness in its white cheek, and a bloodless lip, and scintillating eye. . . ." When she thought Nelly had betrayed her, "a maniac's fury kindled under her brows," and she associated Nelly with witchcraft, saying, "I'll make her howl a recantation!"

DESIRE FULFILLED

After Cathy's death, a period of eighteen years elapsed during which Heathcliff continued to seek the wholeness which had eluded him in incest, yet he did not forsake his incestuous longing. His obsession with the dead Cathy and his desire to have her possess him did not abate, but grew stronger. Heathcliff returned to the bed that he and Cathy had shared until separated by Hindley at age twelve and surrendered to his "soul's bliss." When Nelly found him dead, she tried to close his eyelids to shut out the "life-like gaze of exultation," but "they would not shut," typical of the corpse of a vampire. Hareton and Nelly honored Heathcliff's wish to be buried with his coffin opening into Cathy's, free now that he had shed his mortal being to "dissolve with her." If we are to take seriously the rumors that Heathcliff and Cathy roamed the countryside after his death as adults not children, we must conclude that the union which had been forbidden to them in life found fulfillment in death.

Love and Addiction in *Wuthering Heights*

Debra Goodlett

Author Debra Goodlett writes that the relationship between Catherine and Heathcliff is an unhealthy addiction. She discusses the precursors of addictive behavior—missing parents, a lack of emotional support and outside interests, and the need for love and comfort—and she explains how both Heathcliff and Cathy's lives fit these criteria.

Some scholars explain [Heathcliff and Catherine's] relationship in terms of Romanticism. Volumes of literature containing discussions of Byronic heroes and bleak landscapes have filled entire sections in university libraries. Others speak of the reconciliation of conflicting attractions: the destructive nature of Catherine and Heathcliff's relationship obtains equilibrium in the second generation with Cathy and Hareton. In a similar vein, the theme of another type of duality is proposed: that of the intellect (Lipton), and the heart (Heathcliff). Some believe that Emily Brontë attempted to mesh this duality into one entity, and from that failure arises the intensity and dramatic conflict that exists in *Wuthering Heights*. I would argue instead that this intensity arises out of the bond between Catherine and Heathcliff, a bond which can best be described as an addiction rather than as a "theme" of a traditional Romantic Gothic novel. The addictive nature of the relationship is illuminated by Catherine's cry of "I am Heathcliff!" Lacking any inner resources, Catherine attempts to capture Heathcliff's psyche to fulfill the emptiness in her own soul. This then is sexual addiction—the need to possess another being. While the passionate intensity produced by this conflicting pull between the two lovers has been explained in various ways, these explanations seem fragmentary. Recent developments in psy-

Reprinted from Debra Goodlet, "Love and Addiction in *Wuthering Heights*," *The Midwest Quarterly*, vol. 37, no. 3 (Spring 1996), by permission of the publisher.

chology offer new insights on unresolved literary conflicts, and I believe that Catherine and Heathcliff's relationship may well fit into this category. Exploring this relationship, through a paradigm of addiction, will illuminate this theory.

Stanton Peele, author of *Love and Addiction*, states:

> An addiction exists when a person's attachment to a sensation, an object, or another person is such as to lessen his apprecia- tion of and ability to deal with other things in his environment, or in himself, so that he has become increasingly dependent on that experience as his only source of gratification.

Peele does not differentiate between people or drugs. Both are seen as the focuses of addictions, and in addictive rela- tionships the participants are forced to rely on the other for bolstering their flagging identities. Addictive relationships are based on the need for psychological security; the part- ners, as in a drug addiction, will do everything necessary to maintain that bond. Catherine and Heathcliff unsuccessfully attempt to do this, with tragic results.

Stanton Peele explores relationships resembling Catherine and Heathcliff's and theorizes that many of the environmen- tal factors that are believed to cause drug addictions also play a role in initiating addictive relationships. *Wuthering Heights* contains many of these same conditions, and these are con- tributory to the addictive nature of Catherine and Heathcliff's relationship. Peele states that addiction occurs

> in people who have little to anchor them to life. Lacking an underlying direction, finding few things that can entertain or motivate them, they have nothing to compete with the effects of an addiction for possession of their lives.

THE MISSING PARENTS

This "lack of underlying direction" correlates strongly with an absence of strong parental figures. Catherine is entirely without guiding influences while growing up. Her parents die early in her childhood, and only Hindley, her brother, is left as a possibly stabilizing factor. Given Hindley's nature, which is emotionally sterile, Catherine is still bereft of a pos- itive role model that could give some direction to her life. Even while alive, Catherine's father has difficulty accepting Catherine as she is and repeatedly informs Catherine of his disappointment in her. Mr. Earnshaw tells her during a rare moment of tenderness between them, "Why cannot you al- ways be a good lass, Cathy?" Catherine replies, "Why cannot you always be a good man, father?" Another parental figure, Joseph, consistently influences Mr. Earnshaw to reject Catherine.

> He [Joseph] encouraged him to regard Hindley as a repro-bate; and, night after night, he regularly grumbled out a long string of tales against Heathcliff and Catherine always mind-ing to flatter Earnshaw's weakness by heaping the heaviest blame on the latter.

Similarly, Heathcliff, an orphan prior to his arrival at Wuther-ing Heights, receives only a small amount of affection from the elder Earnshaw before Earnshaw's death, and with his death, both Catherine and Heathcliff are grief-stricken. Nelly Dean describes their sorrow and their isolation:

> I ran to the children's room; their door was ajar, I saw they have never laid down, though it was past midnight; but they were calmer, and did not need me to console them. The little souls were comforting each other with better thoughts than I could have hit on; no parson in the world ever pictured heaven so beautifully as they did, in their innocent talk; and, while I sobbed and listened, I could not help wishing we were all there safe together.

CATHERINE AND HEATHCLIFF LACK EMOTIONAL SUPPORT AND OUTSIDE INTERESTS

Another characteristic indicative of an addictive nature is a lack of emotional stability. Peele believes that a large part of a healthy emotional outlook is the ability to express feelings appropriately. According to most psychologists, the early de-velopmental years are the most critical in the formation of this ability. Catherine and Heathcliff are both punished when young for expressing feelings. Nelly Dean tells of one such incident:

> "Nay, Cathy, I cannot love thee; thou'rt worse than thy brother. Go say thy prayers, child, and ask God's pardon. I doubt thy mother and I must rue that we ever reared thee!" That made her cry at first: and then being repulsed continu-ally hardened her, and she laughed if I told her to say she was sorry for her faults, and beg to be forgiven.

Insularity is another characteristic of an addictive rela-tionship. Wuthering Heights is the epitome of desolation, as symbolized by the savage natural setting. Peele states that "for the children, at least in their early years, the sealing off of the home strictly limited what sense they could make of things on their own." Catherine and Heathcliff live in this isolated environment. Except for Mr. Lockwood, the narrator, there is no mention of visitors to Wuthering Heights. And as was discussed earlier, Catherine and Heathcliff are without emotional support from either parents or siblings. Without any of these external stimuli, neither Catherine nor Heathcliff have the opportunity to develop social dexterity or coping skills.

With these disadvantages, it is not surprising that Catherine and Heathcliff should be attracted to each other; they share similar outlooks. Peele maintains that addictive relationships are defined by the desire to be consumed by love; to form one human entity out of two incomplete beings. Without inner resources, people are driven to look outside of themselves to find those resources, usually in individuals sharing similar outlooks. Catherine and Heathcliff are alike in their passionate rebellious natures, natures unsatisfied by the arti-

---

In Need of Forgiveness

Vereen M. Bell writes that in an atmosphere where "father is turned against son, brother against sister, servant against master, husband against wife, lover against lover," it is clearly the want of forgiveness that "disrupts the moral and social order of Wuthering Heights."

It is the want of forgiveness—or phrased positively, it is vengeance—that disrupts the moral and social order of *Wuthering Heights.* Hindley cannot forgive Heathcliff for usurping the love of his father; so once he is master of the Heights, he sees that Heathcliff is methodically humiliated and degraded. Heathcliff's degradation in turn enforces a physical and psychological separation from Catherine which preordains her marriage to Edgar Linton. When Heathcliff acquires his fortune, he uses the power it affords to avenge himself against Hindley, whom he easily corrupts and destroys; against Hareton and Catherine, the children, who of course are innocent; against Isabella, who is equally blameless; and through all of these, against Edgar Linton, whom he hates not just as a rival but as an embodiment of everything effete and conventional that erodes Catherine's spirit and finally destroys her. Father is turned against son, brother against sister, servant against master, husband against wife, lover against lover—"Every man's hand was against his neighbour."

Vereen M. Bell, "*Wuthering Heights* and the Unforgivable Sin," in Bradford A. Booth, ed., *Nineteenth-Century Fiction.* New York: AMS Reprint Company, 1965.

ficial society that Linton represents. Both are rebellious against societal structures, as demonstrated by the relationship itself. Heathcliff is looked upon as a rough, uncouth savage, and Catherine is attracted by the inherently taboo nature of the bond. Not only is Heathcliff rough, he is also her foster brother, and thus it is also an incestuous bond.

Along with insularity, people in addictive relationships also have few outside interests. Peele believes that the extent and diversity of a person's social relationships and activities are crucial in determining whether a person will become addictive in his or her relationships. As children, Catherine and Heathcliff entertain themselves by taking walks among the moors. Other than this activity, neither displays an interest in hobbies and such things. Along with lack of interest, Heathcliff in particular has no time for anything else as he is kept busy working for Hindley.

This lack of outside interests contributes to the change in quality of Catherine and Heathcliff's relationship. As with any addiction, as tolerance develops, initial feelings of joy may dissipate, but the overwhelming need remains. Catherine states to Nelly in this critical passage:

> So he shall never know I love him: and that, not because he's handsome, Nelly, but because he's more myself than I am. Whatever our souls are made of, his and mine are the same; and Linton's is as different as a moonbeam from lightning, or frost from fire.

At first glance, her speech seems a declaration of love. Catherine states that Heathcliff is a part of her; if Heathcliff were to disappear, then Catherine would no longer exist. This passionate outcry is indicative of the intensity present in Catherine and Heathcliff's relationship. The intensity is not so much an erotic element, but a dependent, life-giving need, without which Catherine or Heathcliff would wither. Very little joy is shown by either of them; instead, both seem usually intense and desperate. As Catherine states, "My love for Heathcliff resembles the eternal rocks beneath; a source of little visible delight, but necessary."

CATHERINE'S NEED FOR LOVE AND COMFORT

Dramatic conflict begins to arise in the novel when, out of loneliness and boredom, Catherine is drawn to the Lintons' active social world. At the time of her first introduction to the Lintons, Catherine is attacked by the Lintons' dog, and she is forced by her injuries to remain in Linton's care; thus begins the conflict in Catherine and Heathcliff's attachment. Catherine begins to find the comfortable, secure atmosphere of Linton's world attractive, and after returning to Wuthering Heights, sees Heathcliff in a new light. Until now, Catherine has seen no other world, and she looks upon the new one as an appealing alternative to the strangling addictive bond that she shares with Heathcliff. Linton can provide her with the material comforts that her insecurity demands. The addiction between Catherine and Heathcliff is complicated by Catherine's need, not only for love, but also for material comfort. To Catherine, psychological security means having not only a partner, but having one that is wealthy and socially acceptable. According to 19th-century custom, a woman was not "complete" unless she married successfully. Heathcliff is barely capable of supplying himself with food and shelter, and so Catherine's eyes stray towards Linton. She is reluctant, due to her intense bond with Heathcliff, but he cannot fulfill her need for comfort and security. Catherine states:

> I've no more business to marry Edgar Linton than I have to be in heaven: and if the wicked man in there had not brought Heathcliff so low, I shouldn't have thought of it. It would degrade me to marry Heathcliff now.

After her marriage to Linton, the following years are tranquil for Catherine. Heathcliff has disappeared, and Catherine attempts, somewhat successfully, to be satisfied with the psychological and material security that Linton provides for her. The one lacking element is the intensity that she shared with Heathcliff. Only upon Heathcliff's return is her addiction again triggered.

She persistently attempts to manipulate Heathcliff's acceptance into the Linton society, and she is temporarily successful. Present in Catherine is the knowledge, demonstrated by Heathcliff's impatience, that the arrangement between Catherine and Heathcliff is not satisfactory. Heathcliff will either possess Catherine or he will destroy the security that Catherine has found in Linton. Catherine, on the other hand, seems content with the knowledge that Heathcliff belongs to her emotionally. It is not necessary that she possess him in a more physical sense. To maintain her denial, Catherine demands that Linton accept Heathcliff as her "friend," regardless of how inappropriate that demand is.

Catherine and Heathcliff's relationship is obviously one of a romantic nature, as has demonstrated by Linton's careful use of the word "friend." Linton states, "will you give up Heathcliff hereafter, or will you give up me? It is impossible for you to be my friend and his at the same time: and I absolutely require to know which you choose."

Catherine is oblivious to the problem here. It is necessary for her to have Heathcliff in her life, at whatever the cost. The addiction is shown most clearly when Catherine is faced with Linton's ultimatum. Catherine has to choose either Linton, and the psychological security inherent in that relationship, or she must choose Heathcliff and the passionate intensity present in the addiction. Forced with this dilemma, Catherine becomes ill. Peele believes that extreme emotional reactions also conclusively establish that a relationship is addictive. Definite signs of withdrawal are displayed when a partner attempts to leave the relationship—signs of physical illness, such as shortness of breath, nausea, and faintness. All of these are demonstrated by addictive lovers upon hints of the relationship being dissolved. Catherine's illness, after Linton's ultimatum, is a direct result of the threat of losing Heathcliff. She is described as having symptoms of weakness, loss of appetite, and faintness.

HEATHCLIFF'S NEED FOR POSSESSION

Heathcliff, unlike Catherine, needs to possess in a physical sense. Confronted with Catherine's rejection of him, she states that it would "degrade" her to marry him, and Heathcliff leaves with the express intention of remaking himself into an image that will satisfy Catherine. Heathcliff is a man without an identity and is relief upon Catherine to choose that identity for him. He returns several years later, a polished, wealthy man.

Upon his return, Heathcliff is faced with the dilemma of Catherine's marriage. He attempts to destroy Catherine's marriage, regardless of what damage that inflicts on her. Furious and in withdrawal, Heathcliff wants only to repossess Catherine. Heathcliff is more honest with his feelings than any other character in the novel. Nowhere does he try to hide how he feels; Heathcliff needs Catherine to survive emotionally. Becoming distraught because of the separation that occurs during Catherine and Linton's marriage, Heathcliff remains dissatisfied until he is again reunited with her; in death, buried beside her. This desire, I believe, is what primarily motivates Heathcliff. According to Peele, "when the connection is severed, even temporarily, the lover ceases to exist—something must retrace it." But Heathcliff has no life, no concerns other than his obsession with Catherine. This is made clear by Heathcliff's statements directly after Catherine's death:

> And I pray one prayer—I repeat it till my tongue stiffens—
> Catherine Earnshaw, may you not rest as I am living! You
> said I killed—you—haunt me, then! The murdered do haunt
> their murderers, I believe. I know that ghosts have wandered
> on earth. Be with me always—take any form—drive me mad!
> Only be not leave me in this abyss, where I cannot find you! I
> cannot live without my soul!

Upon Catherine's death, Heathcliff is finished. He lives several more years, but he is a half-man—a shadow of what a human being should be. He needed Catherine to fill the abyss in his soul.

Heathcliff is more a force than a man. He is passionate, available, loyal, and desires only Catherine. Catherine's own addictive nature readily motivates her into giving her allegiance to Heathcliff. Catherine and Heathcliff's relationship, seen as a separate entity, always stands outside societal standards. Heathcliff's presence is thinly disguised as a childhood friend, but the relationship has always been taboo. This forbidden element, I believe, only adds to the addictive pull the relationship holds. It is stimulated by outside hostility, from Linton and others. The relationship also demands from both partners total attention to the addictive bond. Heathcliff never abandons this theme, but Catherine's failure to totally engross herself in him, as demonstrated by her marriage to Linton, eventually leads to her destruction.

ADDICTIVE LOVE

A healthy love affair demands well-balanced, mature individuals who have the capacity to want the best for the other partner. Catherine and Heathcliff do not display these qualities. Addictive love differs from a healthy attachment by the lover's need to possess the other being, regardless of the effect this might have on the latter. Catherine's love for Linton seems less destructive them does the love that she and Heathcliff share. As Catherine states:

> If all else perished, and he remained, I should still continue to
> be, and if all else remained, and he were annihilated, the uni-
> verse would turn to a mighty stranger; I should not seem a part

of it. My love for Linton is like the foliage in the woods: time will change it, I'm well aware, as winter changes the trees.

Catherine does not exist without Heathcliff. Catherine and Heathcliff nourish their insufficiencies by feeding off each other, and as the novel shows, this system of addiction is not an efficient one.

Peele states that addicts are "emotionally detached from people, and are capable of seeing others only as objects to be exploited." Heathcliff is totally detached from people; he shows no affection for any human being, other than Catherine. He displays hostility towards everyone, except when it is necessary for him to gain some advantage from them. Even with Catherine, he is interested not so much in her well-being but in what the relationship can bring to him. After Heathcliff's return he is outraged to find Catherine has married Linton. Heathcliff's lack of concern for Catherine is exemplified when he states:

> I want you to be aware that I know you have treated me infernally—infernally! Do you hear? And if you flatter yourself that I don't perceive it you are a fool; and if you think I can be consoled by sweet words you are an idiot: and if you fancy I'll suffer unrevenged, I'll convince you of the contrary, in a very little while!

Catherine is similar to Heathcliff in this respect. She uses Nelly Dean as an intermediary for her intrigue with Heathcliff, but otherwise displays no affection towards her. She dislikes her brother, Hindley, and barely tolerates Linton. Her only passion is for Heathcliff, and for what validation he can provide for her femininity. . . .

Peele examines in depth the strikingly close similarity between the pattern drug addiction takes and that of an addictive relationship, and he believes that addiction is addiction, no matter what the focus is. He defines love addiction as an obsessive and destructive relationship, and this correlates perfectly with Catherine and Heathcliff's attachment. Love addiction is based on an unhealthy dependence between two individuals, and Catherine and Heathcliff's relationship is clarified by examining it through this framework of dependency. Their relationship is based upon a lack of inner resources, and not upon love. Their bond is not an amoral one, or outside the realm of human experience either. Rather, it is a pattern of an obsessive and destructive relationship; one that is found frequently in literature and in modern society.

128   *Readings on* Wuthering Heights

REFERENCES

Abrams, M.H. *The Romantic Period: An Introduction, The Norton Anthology of English Literature.* Ed. M.H. Abrams. New York: Norton, 1974. 1–19.

Apter, T.E. "Romanticism and Romantic Love in Wuthering Heights." *The Art of Emily Bronte.* Ed. Anne Smith. London: Vision Press, 1976. 205–22.

Brontë, Emily. *Wuthering Heights.* New York: Washington Square Press, 1964.

Frye, Northrop. *A Study of English Romanticism.* New York: Random House, 1968.

Gold, Linda. "Catherine Earnshaw: Mother and Daughter." *English Journal,* 74.3 (1985), 68–73.

Guerard, Albert J. "Preface to Wuthering Heights." *Twentieth Century Interpretations on Wuthering Heights.* Ed. Maynard Mack. New Jersey: Prentice-Hall, 1968. 63–68.

Peele, Stanton. *Love and Addiction.* New York: Taplinger, 1975.

Reed, Donna K. "The Discontents of Civilization in Wuthering Heights and Buddenbrooks." *Comparative Literature,* 41.3 (1989), 209–22.

Traversi, Derek. "The Brontë Sisters and Wuthering Heights." *Twentieth Century Interpretationis on Wuthering Heights.* Ed. Maynard Mack. New Jersey: Prentice-Hall, 1968. 49–62.

Van Ghent, Dorothy. "On Wuthering Heights." *A Wuthering Heights Handbook.* Ed. Lettis and Morris. New York: Odyssey Press, 1961. 1242.

Suicide in *Wuthering Heights*

Barbara Gates

Barbara Gates of the University of Delaware discusses the theme of suicide in *Wuthering Heights* by pointing to examples of Brontë's evident knowledge of English criminal law, burial rites, and superstition in reference to suicide. On more than one occasion, Brontë's characters cover up suicides to prevent property forfeiture and to allow for Christian burials. But with tempests and hailstorms brewing on the moors, the locals are wary of the bodies beneath the churchyard wall. Suspicious of suicide, they are careful not to tread on these graves.

In *Wuthering Heights* much of the plot turns upon the rights of ownership to the Heights and the Grange, especially to the entail of the lands of the Grange. . . . Brontë seems to have been well informed about the history of English criminal laws governing suicide; she also knew in intimate detail the folklore associated with self-destruction. Both her plot and her imaginative envisioning of the deaths of her first-generation characters hinge upon her fictional use of this knowledge. As I hope to show, Heathcliff's claim to Wuthering Heights depends on his concealing his own conviction that Hindley's death is suicidal; Catherine's burial place under the churchyard wall may have been determined by the nature of her death, just as her haunting of Heathcliff is definitely in accord with folk beliefs surrounding a questionable death like hers; and Heathcliff's own care not to seem suicidal may in large part be accounted for by his own overwhelming desire to be buried in the churchyard next to Catherine.

Eighteenth- and early nineteenth-century suicide law can be summarized briefly. Those laws that would have been op-

Excerpted from Barbara Gates, "Suicide and *Wuthering Heights*," *The Victorian Newsletter*, Fall 1976. Used by permission of the author.

erative during the time of the action of *Wuthering Heights* (1771–1803) still dated from the tenth century, when civil law required both the ignominious burial of a suicide (with a stake through his heart and in the public highway, customarily at a crossroad) and the forfeiture of his personal and real property to the Crown. The *felo-de-se*, as the suicide was called, was to be impaled and buried outside of consecrated ground because his was thought to be a crime against God. . . . He was to lose his goods and properties because it was believed that suicide could be prevented if the *felo-de-se* knew of the harsh and inevitable consequences for his heirs. Forfeiture was further justified because at one time suicide was not considered a crime in and of itself, but instead a form of confession to some other crime deserving of punishment. . . .

In 1823, when Emily Brontë was just five and Patrick Brontë was officiating at Thornton, a new statute was passed making it unlawful to bury a *felo-de-se* in the public highway. A coroner was to order the body to be buried privately between the hours of nine and twelve at night in a churchyard or other burial ground, without a stake driven through his body but also without the rights of Christian burial. Forfeiture would remain legal until 1870.

A PROPER BURIAL FOR AN IMPROPER DEATH

In *Wuthering Heights* Brontë seems to have felt free to use both the laws in effect during the time of her story and those governing early Victorian times. In narrating the details surrounding Hindley's death (1784), for example, she draws upon the earlier statutes. Although the exact cause of Hindley's death is never determined, all who saw him at the end claim that he died in a state of drunkeness. Mr. Kenneth, who tells Nelly about the death, says that he "died true to his character, drunk as a lord." And Heathcliff, when Nelly requests whether she may proceed with suitable arrangements for Hindley's funeral, retorts:

> Correctly . . . that fool's body should be buried at the crossroads, without ceremony of any kind. I happened to leave him ten minutes, yesterday afternoon; and, in that interval, he fastened the two doors of the house against me, and he has spent the night in drinking himself to death deliberately!

The precise circumstances of Hindley's death, which are reported in considerable detail, have important implications for the course of the novel. For if Hindley did die drunk and debauched, as both Kenneth and Heathcliff indicate he did, in the eighteenth century he would automatically have been considered a suicide, exactly as Heathcliff suggests. Even more importantly, in that case his property legally should have been forfeited to the Crown, with nothing left for Hareton and hence nothing left for Heathcliff to employ as a tool in his revenge. It is probably for this reason that Heathcliff allows Nelly to perform proper burial rights for Hindley, thus relinquishing a more immediate revenge upon Hindley's dead body while gaining a long-term hold on the entire Earnshaw family.

Earlier, just before coming to the Heights, Nelly had consulted with Linton's lawyer about Hindley's death and had requested that the lawyer come to the Heights with her. His refusal is also telling, for he advises "that Heathcliff be let alone, affirming, if the truth were known, Hareton would be found little else than a beggar." The "truth" here may be that Heathcliff is Hareton's only hope because he is Hindley's creditor or that the lawyer, probably Mr. Green, is already under Heathcliff's influence. But it may also be that Hindley's death, as a suicide, is better left ignored, primarily because of the possibility of forfeiture.

A Ghost in the Mirror

Catherine's death precedes her brother's by only half a year, and it too can be considered suicidal. There is little doubt that Catherine knows how to induce her own ill health, although, when she first embarks upon her fast in chapter XI, she does not intend suicide. At this point totally breaking her own body and heart is, for Catherine, still "a deed to be reserved for a forlorn hope." What happens, however, is that Catherine's body only partially cooperates with her will, and Nelly's assumption that Catherine is in total control of her situation is one of Nelly's tragic miscalculations. After only three days' fast, Catherine is already past saving. When she realizes that neither Linton nor Heathcliff has become genuinely alarmed and then chooses not to die, she cannot reverse her headlong journey toward destruction.

The important scene before her mirror already spells this doom for Catherine. . . . Catherine is shocked when she sees her own reflection because she seems to understand what Yorkshire folklore dictates: that sick people should never look at themselves in the mirror. If they do, their souls may take flight from their weak bodies by being projected into the mirror, and this can cause their imminent death. In accordance with this belief, immediately after she sees her reflection in the mirror, Catherine is convinced that she really will die. Q.D. Leavis suggests that this realization replaces Catherine's fear of ghosts, anxiously expressed just before: "I hope it will not come out when you are gone! Oh! Nelly, the room is haunted!"

I believe, however, that the realization and the fear are even more closely related. For Catherine actually seems to consider *herself* to be the ghost, once she recognizes that hers is the face in the mirror. "'Myself,' she gasped, 'and the clock is striking twelve! It's true then; that's dreadful!'" Her utter horror here stems from Catherine's superstitious belief that suicides, and she now assumes herself to be a suicide, become ghosts. This is why custom, and then law, would have them buried with stakes through their hearts—to prevent their walking. It is then this aspect of Catherine's unnerving realization before the mirror that incites her subsequent raving about the ghosts at Gimmerton Kirkyard, while she addresses Heathcliff about their past and their future.

> It's a rough journey, and a sad heart to travel it; and we must pass by Gimmerton Kirk, to go that journey! We've braved its ghosts often together, and dared each other to stand among the graves and ask them to come. But Heathcliff, if I dare you now, will you venture? If you do, I'll keep you. I'll not lie there by myself; they may bury me twelve feet deep, and throw the church down over me, but I won't rest till you are with me. I never will!

After this scene, there is only one more meeting between Catherine and Heathcliff before her actual death. On that occasion their dialogue is filled with further allusions to Catherine's suicide and her would-be haunting of Heathcliff. Catherine now feels that she will never be at peace; while Heathcliff repeatedly expresses regret over what he feels is Catherine's self-murder and his relationship to it:

> You have killed yourself. Yes, you may kiss me, and cry; and wring out my kisses and tears. They'll blight you—they'll damn you. You loved me—then what *right* had you to leave me? What right—answer me—for the poor fancy you felt for Linton? Because misery, and degradation, and death, and nothing that God or Satan could inflict would have parted us, *you*, of your own will, did it. I have not broken your heart—*you* have broken it—and in breaking it, you have broken

mine. So much the worse for me, that I am strong. Do I want to live? What kind of living will it be when you—Oh, God! would *you* like to live with your soul in the grave? . . .

CURSES, TEMPESTS, AND HAILSTORMS

Like Hindley, Catherine is not buried as a suicide. Nelly wonders "after the wayward and impatient existence she had led, whether she merited a haven of peace at last," but after looking at her in death, decides that she probably does. Catherine is interred in the corner of the Kirkyard under the wall, "to the surprise of the villagers." Since the local people did not know of the means of Catherine's death, they had expected that she would be buried either in the chapel with the Lintons or by the tombs of the Earnshaws. Their wonderment is therefore quite understandable, especially when one recalls another folk belief about suicides. Particularly after the 1823 law, when suicides could legally be buried in churchyards, it became customary in parts of northern Britain for their bodies to be laid below the churchyard wall, so that no one would be likely to walk over their graves. Pregnant women, for example, had to be particularly careful not to tred over the grave of a suicide, for it was thought that doing so would cause miscarriage. The place of Catherine's burial would thus have had particular significance for the folk of Gimmerton, who would no doubt have inferred the nature of her death from the location of her grave. Since they would also have known that Catherine gave birth to young Catherine before her death, the superstition about miscarriage would have gained considerable force in the case of her grave.

With regard to Catherine's death, Brontë draws on one final custom when she has the weather change so suddenly immediately after the funeral. Again in accord with folk belief, the corpses of suicides were expected to produce tempests or hailstorms once they made contact with the earth. In Catherine's case, Nelly tells us that there is just such a change in weather after Catherine is interred: "That Friday made the last of our fine days, for a month. In the evening, the weather broke; the wind shifted from south to northeast, and brought rain first, and then sleet and snow.". . .

HEATHCLIFF'S FINAL WISHES

Unquestionably the place of Catherine's burial determines Heathcliff's own choice of a burial site and consequently his own need not to become discovered as a suicide. Because of his reputation and his doubtful place in the Gimmerton community, it is far less likely that Heathcliff would be extended the kind of pity that had allowed for the churchyard burials of Hindley and Catherine. He knows this and knows too of the possibility of interment in the public highway and is therefore scrupulous about not appearing suicidal. . . . Unfortunately for Heathcliff's union with Catherine, Linton dies before Heathcliff does and is the one to be buried in the grave next to hers. Lawyer Green, now the tool of Heathcliff, does suggest that Linton should appropriately be buried in the chapel. Linton's death is of natural causes and his family all lie there. But Green, even though under Heathcliff's influence, must abide by the stipulations of Linton's will, which states Linton's desire to be buried with Catherine. . . .

Less than a year elapses between Linton's death and Heathcliff's, the year in which Heathcliff and Wuthering Heights are so intensely haunted by Catherine that even the prosaic Lockwood is influenced to dream of her. Toward the end of this time, Nelly observes how isolated and peculiar Heathcliff has become and warns him against taking his own life. As she notes, he undergoes his most dramatic set of changes from the time of his curious hunting accident, when "his gun burst while out on the hills by himself." Whether or not the accident is a failed suicide attempt, to which Heathcliff may have been driven by the extremity of his mental state and his desire for Catherine, cannot be discerned. . . . "I cannot continue in this condition," he tells Nelly, "I have to remind myself to breathe—almost to remind my heart to beat!" He also forgets to eat but makes the attempt when Nelly urges him and takes great care to tell her that "It is not my fault, that I cannot eat or rest. . . . I assure you it is through no settled designs."

As he begins to fail, the one thing uppermost in Heathcliff's mind is his burial. To Nelly he gives detailed instructions for its procedures:

> You remind me of the manner that I desire to be buried in. It is to be carried to the churchyard, in the evening. . . . No minister need come; nor need anything be said over me.

Each of Heathcliff's requests is absolutely in accord with the 1823 statute governing the burial of suicides: the hour, the place, and the lack of a Christian burial service; and Nelly seems to realize their significance. In a moment of insight she brings up the fear that has haunted Heathcliff ever since the day of Catherine's death:

> "And supposing you persevered in your obstinate fast, and died by that means, and they refused to bury you in the precincts of the Kirk?" I said, shocked at his godless indifference. "How would you like it?"

Heathcliff's only means of recourse now are to charge Nelly with the business of moving his body, so that he can be with Catherine, and directly to threaten Nelly with haunting should she fail to comply. The threat seems sufficient to frighten the somewhat superstitious servant, and the next evening, when Heathcliff does die, Nelly is very careful to interfere with Kenneth's decision as to the cause of death:

> Kenneth was perplexed to pronounce of what disorder the master died. I concealed the fact of his having swallowed nothing for four days, fearing it might lead to trouble, and then, I am persuaded he did not abstain on purpose; it was the consequence of his strange illness, not the cause.

GHOSTS ON THE MOORS

Her actions now free Nelly to carry out Heathcliff's instructions to the letter and "to the scandal of the whole neighborhood." Shocked not only by Heathcliff's interment side by side with the married Lintons, the people seem also to know the meaning of Heathcliff's burial without Christian rites. It is not long afterward that under the Nab the local shepherd boy sees the ghosts of what he must now consider as two suicides, Heathcliff and Catherine.

In the end, Lockwood's much-discussed final words take on added irony when the folklore of suicide is regarded. Referring to the gravesites of Catherine, Linton, and Heathcliff, Lockwood wonders "how anyone could ever imagine unquiet slumbers for the sleepers in that quiet earth." But anyone knowing the customs surrounding suicide in eighteenth- and nineteenth-century Britain—as Emily Brontë did—could, on the contrary, hardly imagine quiet slumbers for them.

The Anorexics of *Wuthering Heights*

Giuliana Giobbi

Critic Giuliana Giobbi of Rome, Italy, explores the theme of anorexia, or self-starvation in *Wuthering Heights*. The characters of Isabella Linton, Catherine Earnshaw, and finally Heathcliff are all afflicted, to some degree, with self-starvation. Giobbi writes that the pathological process of anorexia brings women (and men) to the verge of madness and death. "Killed by something within themselves," she says Brontë's anorexic characters' "souls with their bodies into a slow and painful death by starvation."

The impact of a psychological syndrome upon a literary work may have many—explicit and implicit—consequences. Biographical input, social conditioning, self-conscious threads are bound to enrich the fictional texts, thus eliciting new and thought-provoking critical interpretations .

This is certainly the case with anorexia, a form of self-starvation which is spreading in the whole of the Western world, mostly among the female population. . . .

Situated in the complex period of adolescence, anorexia is a wilful self-starvation which strikes girls who are dissatisfied with their bodies and probably wish to stop their growth so as to delay and escape the trauma of becoming an adult woman and facing up to life. Recently, physicians have defined the anorexic girl as one who 'is trying desperately not to grow up. Her body is becoming a woman's, against her will. That's got to be stopped.'

In this turmoil of adolescence, the choice of starvation can be interpreted at the same time as a sign of depression, and as a form of rebellion: anorexia somehow satisfies the girl's need to be 'special'. Indeed, it is not as if this disorder 'strikes' the girl, because she takes an active part in it. Para-

Excerpted from Giuliana Giobbi, "'No Bread Will Feed My Hungry Soul': Anorexic Heroines in Female Fiction, from the Example of Emily Brontë as Mirrored by Anita Brookner, Gianna Schelotto, and Alessandra Arachi," *Journal of European Studies*, vol. 27, no. 105 (March 1997), pp. 73–89. Used by permission of the publisher.

doxically, it is the girl's need to be emancipated and independent which generates anorexia. Forced to admit her loneliness and her difficulty in adapting to her peers, the girl feels depressed and alienated from the others; she takes on an imaginary feeling of guilt and denies herself any pleasure and any contact with the world as if to punish herself. In transforming her body and winning the battle of denial against desire, the anorexic woman hopes to control her emotional needs too. . . .

Food and fire, together with all the detailed rituals of domestic routine, are important realistic elements of the passionately original novel written by Emily Brontë a year before her death, namely, *Wuthering Heights* (1847). Catherine's impossible love for the wild, mysterious Heathcliff can be read as an adult woman's tragic yearning to return to her 'half savage, and hardy, and free' childhood in the Yorkshire moors.

The leitmotif of starvation recurs throughout the novel, like the chorus of a classical Greek tragedy. Love, depression, neurosis, lead in turn Isabella Linton, the heroine Catherine Earnshaw and, finally, Heathcliff himself, to deprive themselves of food and human company. Human passions are heightened to a hectic degree in their intensity, and the nature of both Catherine and Heathcliff remains untamed to the very end. As Gilbert and Gubar suggest,— Catherine's 'education in doubleness, in ladylike decorum meaning also ladylike decent, is marked by an actual doubling or fragmentation of her personality'. Thus, Heathcliff might be seen as her 'id', her rebellious alter-ego (see the significant image of the 'whip' chosen as a present by young Catherine). According to this perspective, Heathcliff's literal starvation leading to his death would parallel Catherine's dangerous spiritual starvation. Anxious self-denial and uncertainty about one's own identity are the ultimate products of a female education, Brontë seems to imply.

'Oh, I will die', she exclaimed, 'since no one cares anything about me.'

Catherine's temperament is a mixture of haughtiness, egocentrism—see the above-quoted words—and stubbornness. In the words of the 'sensible' servant/narrator Ellen Dean, she is 'mischievous and wayward' already as a little child. Significantly, Catherine is attributed wildness, passion and obstinacy throughout the story. The vocabulary used in describing her actions implies violence and insanity. The strength of these definitions increases with the progress of her rapid sickening and deadly decline—which reminds us, in several traits, of Emily's own tragic consumption. After the disappearance of Heathcliff, Catherine falls in a state of 'agitation': she has clearly no control over her passions, and is described as 'wearisome', 'headstrong', 'passionate' and 'haughty'. The doctor himself says she 'would not bear crossing much'. Frenzy is followed by gloom and silence—according to the symptomatology of the manic-depressive syndrome—and all the prerequisites for the onset of anorexia are already there: isolation, stubbornness, intelligence, feelings of guilt. Catherine's marriage to Edgar Linton, moreover, locks her into a conformist social system, and her pregnancy is feared and undesired, an ultimate end of her pristine irresponsibility. Catherine returns to her free childhood self by indulging in tantrums, wheedling and manipulating. Catherine's *malaise* is easily diagnosed as an access of madness, an instance of 'brain fever': her irritable nerves, shaken reason and 'wild, eager eyes' imply Catherine's desperate progress along her downward spiral of self-starvation.

> The thing that irks me most is this shattered prison, after all. I'm tired, tired of being enclosed here.

In a way, Catherine—like Isabella before her—tries to escape her imprisonment in the roles and houses imposed by patriarchy by running away (in the moors so dear to Emily Brontë), by starving herself and, finally, by dying. . . .

OUTBURSTS AND SILENCE: CATHERINE AND HEATHCLIFF'S DECLINE

Renate Gockel writes,

> Women suffering from eating disorders fear being discovered. They need distance so as not to be seen as they really are: frail, needy beings who dread being rejected and not receiving what they wish. Convinced as they are that, in order to get a little love, one must be 'good enough', they try to become as they believe they should be in order to be worthy of love: namely, useful, strong, trustworthy, intelligent persons. If someone breaks their protective barrier and sees them as they really are, they are afraid they will be rejected and abandoned.

Behind Catherine's 'mad scenes' . . . the palpable emotional weakness of the anorexic heroine soon comes to the fore of the narrative scene. Catherine . . . realizes that no one loves her with the intensity she wishes for. In order to 'keep affection alive' . . . Catherine finally gives herself up to suicidal tendencies. . . . Unable to behave 'normally' since she was a child, Catherine loosens the chains of conformist behaviour and bourgeois moderation and lives up to her fame (as created by the negative definitions used by Nelly Dean) finally reaching a climax of tragic, feverish unconsciousness which is nearer to death than to life. . . .

The pathological progress of anorexia brings women on the verge of madness and death: the cases of Catherine and Heathcliff are exemplary, even though they are complicated by other elements—Catherine's fear of pregnancy is set off against Heathcliff's *cupio mori*. Both characters, however, seem to be killed by something within themselves. Their souls will their bodies into a slow and painful death by starvation. . . .

We find Catherine confiding to Nelly her secret, irrational, and inexplicable passion for Heathcliff, and finally giving vent to her desperation in an outburst of passion which preludes her death. The power Catherine retains over the other characters throughout the novel—starting from her ghostly appearance to Mr Lockwood down to her haunting Heathcliff through dreams and through her eponymous daughter—is due to her lack of measure, to the unprecedented, boundless intensity of her feelings.

> Well might Catherine deem that Heaven would be a land of exile to her, unless, with her mortal body, she cast away her mortal character also. Her present countenance had a wild vindictiveness in its white cheek, and a bloodless lip and scintillating eye; and she retained, in her closed fingers, a portion of the locks she had been grasping.

In contrast with Catherine's impetuosity, the slow decline of Heathcliff—meant both on a physical and on a psychological level is characterized by depression and weakness. Heathcliff tries to join dead Catherine by following her along the anorexic path towards starvation. He has a grim, troubled aspect, and is fond of 'continued solitude'. Indeed, Heathcliff loses his will to life, and his behaviour rests on the verge of a melancholy madness, without the devastating rage of Cathy's outbursts.

> I have to remind myself to breathe—almost to remind my heart to beat! And it is like bending back a stiff spring (...) I have a single wish, and my whole being and faculties are yearning to attain it.

Heathcliff's protracted abstinence from food is a case apart: hyper-sensitivity, emulation of Catherine and a clear suicidal wish push him to starve himself to death. But there is in Heathcliff a masculine pride and a silent arrogance even in choosing to meet death on his own terms, without any help from other people. The whole trend of his agony is marked by a will power and determination which denote a demonic stubbornness and an absolute idealism. These circumstances differentiate Heathcliff from the female victims of anorexia. There are no rules for him to break, since he makes his own rules: nothing worldly worries him, and his self-reliance has no limits. Nothing is farther away from the inner emptiness of the anorexic girl, who lacks an integrated ego and cannot attain a psychological integrity. In fact, as Susie Orbach explains, the anorexic woman

> . . . is trying to legitimate herself, to eke out a space, to bring dignity where dismissal and indignity were life (...) Her self-denial is in effect a protest against the rules that circumscribe a woman's life, a demand that she has an absolute right to exist. . . .

The Impoverished, Anorexic Heroine

Whether we follow the traditional interpretation of anorexia as a psychological disease caused by a set of environmental and individual features, or choose the more attractive hypothesis of a social female protest, we must acknowledge the complexity and the dangerousness of this syndrome, which, even if treated, can produce lasting negative consequences in the psyche of the victim. Wolf writes:

> Where feminism taught women to put a higher value on ourselves, hunger teaches us how to erode our self-esteem (...) The more financially independent, in control of events, educated and sexually autonomous women become in the world, the more impoverished, out of control, foolish, and sexually insecure we are asked to feel in our bodies. Hunger makes women feel poor and think poor.

The self-denying mentality induced by self-starvation impoverishes the female victim; her asocial tendency separates her from the others; . . .There is no way out from the closed circuit of denial and control, and no measure in the choice of isolation. Catherine loves too much, and her passion borders on obsession. . . . The inner void of the anorexic woman debars her from a communion with another person; their strong imagination makes all reality unpalatable and incomplete. Robin Norwood, author of *Women Who Love Too Much*, writes:

The more we depend on alcohol, drugs, or food, the more guilt, shame, fear and self-hate we feel. Increasingly lonely and isolated, we may become desperate for the reassurance a relationship with a man seems to promise. Because we feel terrible about ourselves, we want a man to make us feel better. Because we can't love ourselves, we need him to convince us that we are lovable (...) As long as we are bent on escaping ourselves and avoiding our pain, we stay sick.

In conclusion, we may say that our analysis of fictional texts in the perspective of anorexia as an act of extraordinary desperation and courage enriches our understanding of the female psyche.

In this light, the singularity of Emily Brontë's story assumes extremely modern undertones, Catherine is not only a passionate romantic heroine, but also a young woman who is afraid of growing up and wishes to escape from the imprisoning walls of bourgeois patriarchy.

CHRONOLOGY

1812

The Reverend Patrick Brontë marries Maria Branwell.

1814

Maria Brontë is born.

1815

Elizabeth Brontë is born.

1816

Charlotte Brontë is born.

1817

Patrick Branwell Brontë is born.

1818

Emily Jane Brontë is born on July 30.

1820

Anne Brontë is born; the Brontë family moves to the parsonage at Haworth.

1821

Mrs. Brontë dies of cancer; the children's aunt, Elizabeth Branwell, takes over the Brontë household.

1824

In November, Emily joins her sisters at the Clergy Daughters' School at Cowan Bridge.

1825

Maria and Elizabeth contract tuberculosis while away at school; both girls die, and Charlotte and Emily are withdrawn from the school and educated at home until they return to school as teenagers.

1826

Reverend Brontë's gift of wooden soldiers for his son becomes the impetus of the children's imaginative writings; Charlotte and Branwell begin the so-called Angrian stories.

1831

Charlotte attends Roe Head School but returns home seven months later to oversee her sisters' education; Emily and Anne begin to create the Gondal saga.

1835

Charlotte returns to Roe Head School as a governess; Emily, age seventeen, accompanies her but remains only three months due to homesickness.

1837

Emily becomes governess at Law Hill School in Halifax; she remains six months.

1838

Charlotte leaves her post at Roe Head School; Emily writes over half of her surviving poems during the next four years.

1839

Anne and Charlotte hold separate governess positions but leave them within the year.

1840

Anne, Charlotte, and Emily live together at Haworth.

1841

Anne and Charlotte take on new governess positions; the Brontë sisters make unrealized plans to open their own school.

1842

Charlotte and Emily study at the Pensionnat Héger in Brussels; both girls are offered student teacher positions but must return to England when their aunt, Elizabeth Branwell, dies in November.

1843

Patrick joins Anne in York as a tutor; Charlotte returns to Brussels; Emily remains alone with her father at Haworth; the period is one of creativity for her.

1844

Emily arranges her poems into "Gondalan" and "non-Gondalan" manuscripts.

1845

Charlotte discovers Emily's poetry and suggests that she publish a collection along with her own work and Anne's.

1846

The Brontë sisters' poems, *Poems by Currer, Ellis and Acton Bell* are published by Aylott and Jones; Emily's *Wuthering Heights* and Anne's novel *Agnes Grey* are completed and accepted for publication; Charlotte begins work on *Jane Eyre*.

1847

Wuthering Heights, Agnes Grey, and *Jane Eyre* are published.

1848

Anne's novel *The Tenant of Wildfell Hall* is published; Anne's publisher tries to sell the book in American markets under Charlotte's pseudonym, Currer Bell, due to the popularity of *Jane Eyre*; publishers express confusion over the identity of the three Bell authors; in the fall Branwell dies of tuberculosis; Emily succumbs to the same illness on December 19.

1849

Anne dies of tuberculosis; Charlotte's novel *Shirley* is published.

1850

Charlotte becomes the editor of Anne's and Emily's work; new editions of *Agnes Grey* and *Wuthering Heights* are released with some of the sisters' poetry and a "Biographical Notice" by Charlotte.

1854

Charlotte marries A.B. Nicholls.

1855

Charlotte dies during pregnancy.

1861

Brontë's father dies.

FOR FURTHER RESEARCH

BIBLIOGRAPHIES

Janet M. Barclay, *Emily Brontë Criticism 1900–1982: An Annotated Checklist.* Westport, CT: Meckler, 1984.

R.W. Crump, *Charlotte and Emily Brontë: A Reference Guide.* Boston: G.K. Hall, 1982.

Peter Miles, Wuthering Heights: *The Critics Debate Series.* London: Macmillan, 1990.

Anne Passal, *Charlotte and Emily Brontë: An Annotated Bibliography.* New York: Garland, 1979.

BIOGRAPHIES

Juliet Barker, *The Brontës.* London: Weidenfeld and Nicolson, 1994.

Richard Benvenuto, *Emily Brontë.* Boston: Twayne, 1982.

Edward Chitham, *A Life of Emily Brontë.* Oxford: Basil Blackwell, 1987.

Stevie Davies, *Emily Brontë: The Artist as a Free Woman.* Manchester: Charanet Press, 1983.

Barbara and Gareth Lloyd Evans, *The Scribner Companion to the Brontës.* New York: Scribner, 1982.

Katherine Frank, *Chainless Soul: A Life of Emily Brontë.* Boston: Houghton Mifflin, 1990.

Norman Sherry, *Literary Critiques: Charlotte and Emily Brontë.* New York: Arco, 1970.

Muriel Spark and Derek Stanford, *Emily Brontë: Her Life and Work.* New York: London House and Maxwell, 1960.

CRITICISM

Harold Bloom, ed., *Major Literary Characters: Heathcliff.* New York: Chelsea House, 1993.

———, *Modern Critical Interpretations: Emily Brontë's* Wuthering Heights. New York: Chelsea House, 1987.

———, *Modern Critical Views: The Brontës.* New York:

Chelsea House, 1987.

Charlotte Brontë, "Biographical Notice of Ellis and Acton Bell," *Wuthering Heights.* New York: Random House, 1943, pp. xi–xiv.

Alastair Everitt, ed., Wuthering Heights: *An Anthology of Criticism.* London: Frank Cass, 1967.

Ian Gregor, *The Brontës: A Collection of Critical Essays.* Englewood Cliffs, NJ: Prentice-Hall, 1970.

Barbara Hardy, Wuthering Heights: *Emily Brontë.* Oxford: Basil Blackwell, 1963.

Graham Holderness, *Wuthering Heights.* Open Guides to Literature Series. Philadelphia: Open University Press, 1985.

U.C. Knoepflmacher, *Emily Brontë:* Wuthering Heights. Cambridge: Cambridge University Press, 1989.

Rod Mengham, *Emily Brontë:* Wuthering Heights. New York: Penguin Books, 1988.

Linda H. Peterson, *Emily Brontë:* Wuthering Heights. Case Studies in Contemporary Criticism Series. Boston: Bedford Books, 1992.

Lyn Pykett, *Emily Brontë.* Women Writers Series. London: Macmillan, 1989.

Elaine Showalter, *A Literature of Their Own: British Women Novelists from Brontë to Lessing.* Princeton, NJ: Princeton University Press, 1977.

Irene Tayler, *Holy Ghosts: The Male Muses of Charlotte and Emily Brontë.* New York: Columbia University Press, 1990.

Nicola Thompson, "The Unveiling of Ellis Bell: Gender and the Reception of *Wuthering Heights,*" *Women's Studies,* vol. 24, no. 4, March 1995.

Tomas Vogler, ed., *Twentieth-Century Interpretations of* Wuthering Heights. Englewood Cliffs, NJ: Prentice-Hall, 1968.

Virginia Woolf, "*Jane Eyre* and *Wuthering Heights,*" *The Common Reader: First Series.* New York: Harcourt Brace, 1925, pp. 159–65.

LETTERS

Clement Shorter, ed., *The Brontës: Life and Letters.* London: Hodder and Stroughton, 1969.

Thomas James Wise and John Alexander Symington, eds., *The Brontës: Their Lives, Friendships, and Correspondence.* Oxford: Basil Blackwell, 1980.

ABOUT BRONTË'S TIME

Richard Foulkes, *Church and Stage in Victorian England.* Cambridge: Cambridge University Press, 1997.

Sally Mitchell, *Daily Life in Victorian England.* Westport, CT: Greenwood Press, 1996.

John Newenham Summerson, *The Architecture of Victorian London.* New York: Norton, 1971.

Joan Perkin, *Victorian Women.* New York: New York University Press, 1995.

WORKS BY EMILY BRONTË

Poems by Currer, Ellis and Acton Bell (1846)

Wuthering Heights (1847)

PUBLISHED POSTHUMOUSLY

The Complete Poems of Emily Jane Brontë

Five Essays Written in French by Emily Jane Brontë

Gondal's Queen: A Novel in Verse

INDEX

Ackroyd, Tabitha, 80
Agnes Grey, (Anne Brontë) 21
anorexia, 136–37
 and Emily Brontë, 14

Bell, Currer, 21, 22
Bell, Ellis, 21, 22
Bell, Vereen M., 79, 122
Benvenuto, Richard, 14, 15, 16, 20
Branwell, Elizabeth, 13, 14, 18
Brontë, Anne (sister), 13–14, 77
 published work of, 21
 writings of, 15
Brontë, Branwell (brother), 14, 15, 17, 22
Brontë, Charlotte (sister), 13, 18
 apology/defense for *Wuthering Heights,* 73–74
 censorship of Emily's work by, 77
 description of characters by, 75–76, 78
 description of Emily by, 24, 74, 75
 published work of, 21
 reveals Emily's authorship,

22–23
 on second preface, 96–97
Brontë, Elizabeth (sister), 13
Brontë, Emily
 birth/schooling, 13–14
 Catherine's death
  compared to death of, 137–38
 on choice of narrators, 47–49
 death/unveiling authorship of, 22–23
 described by Charlotte, 24, 74, 75
 early writings of, 14–16
 on Heathcliff's character, 60
 and knowledge of monomania, 103
 lacks conventionality, 79–80
 published poetry of, 19, 20–21
 relationship with nature, 16–17
 sexual identity of, 77
 teaching career, 17–18
 use of suicide laws by, 129, 130
 see also Wuthering Heights
Brontë, Maria (mother), 13